Brain-storming

Dynamic
New
Way
to
Create
Successful
Ideas

by
Charles
H.
Clark

Melvin Powers
Wilshire Book Company

12015 Sherman Road, No. Hollywood, CA 91605

To My Teachers
Alex F. Osborn
Willard A. Pleuthner
J. Donald Phillips

A Teacher affects eternity . . . he can never tell where his influence stops. HENRY ADAMS

ACKNOWLEDGMENTS

The author here thanks his friends for the discussions which clarified many points developed in this book.

I owe a special debt to Alex Osborn, for my association with him inspired me to develop my creative powers. Alex believes in people so that they willingly use their hidden capacities. As the father of brainstorming he has produced a "social invention" whose potentialities we are just starting to realize.

Willard Pleuthner and I have appeared together on many programs. Bill's many friends will recognize his influence upon my thinking.

Don Phillips provides us with a way to unleash the creative powers of large groups with his "social invention," Discussion 66. His Hillsdale College seminar on human relations and the Discussion 66 technique changed my whole approach to working with individuals in groups.

Many persons have contributed to my thinking on this topic. The following friends will note traces of our past conversations in this book: Professor John Arnold of Stanford University; Lester R. Bittel of *Factory Management;* Lee H. Bristol, Jr., of Bristol-Myers Company; Dr. Francis A. Cartier of Headquarters, Air Force ROTC; Glenn R. Cowan of B. F. Goodrich Company; Robert T. Early, Jr., of Eastern Gas and Fuel Associates; R. R. Faller, Ethyl Corporation; Dr. James E. Gates of the University of Georgia; A. Scott Hamilton, Jr., John J. McCarthy, and David Purdy of the General Electric Company; Arthur H. Houseknecht of Standard Oil Company of New Jersey; David Hill of Hercules Powder Company; Edward J. Holder of Continental Can Company; Lieutenant Colonel William H. Hunt, U. S. Army; Edwin J. MacEwan of the Greater Paterson Chamber of Commerce; William H. Meskill of the Lago Oil & Transport Company, Ltd.; Donald C. Mitchell of BBDO; Dr. Wilson Nolen of the Harvard Business School; Dr. Sidney J. Parnes of the University of Buffalo; Fred Peterson of the Creole Petroleum Corporation; Harold B. Schmidhauser of the American Management Association; Whitt N. Schultz of the Illinois Bell Telephone Company; Walter J. Tait of the Standard Oil Company of California; Douglas Thomson of United States Rubber Company; Dr. G. Herbert True of the University of Notre Dame; and Charles S. Whiting of McCann-Erickson, Inc.

Some friends gave me encouragement when I needed it most. I especially want to thank for their support Kenneth R. Balsley, Richard R. Crow, Dr. Elliot Danzig, John B. Fox, Philip Gadsden, Jr., Louis Lerda, Dr. Harry Mikami, S. Rowland Morgan, Jr., Cloyd S. Steinmetz, Farrell Toombs, Charlotte Voorhis, and Mrs. Howard Wood, Jr.

I might never have written this book if John Cocci of the Office of Industrial Relations of the Department of the Navy had not invited me to the Pentagon to give my demonstration. His vision in seeing the usefulness of brainstorming for national defense set off a chain reaction of events which resulted in this book. He also made it possible for one of his associates, Joseph T. Davis, to be trained so that he might introduce creative thinking to Navy bureaus and to other branches of our national government.

Last, a word of thanks to Don Murray for his invaluable writing and editorial assistance.

CONTENTS

FOREWORD   15

THE DIFFERENCE AN IDEA MAKES   21

how ideas make a difference
how ideas can change your life
ideas which have made a difference in our world
importance of ideas to the individual, the company, community,
and nation

THE STORK DOESN'T BRING THEM   37

how you give birth to ideas
how the subconscious works
a test to show how your subconscious creates ideas
the practical results of impractical ideas
how creative people have harnessed their subconscious
how you can do the same

BRAINSTORMING? WHAT'S THAT?   49

history of brainstorming
problems of old-style conferences
how brainstorming can solve many of them
how you can brainstorm
some cash results of brainstorming
leading organizations which are using brainstorming
reasons individuals and groups should both use brainstorming

MIXING THE WITCH'S BREW   67

how you can set up a classic brainstorm session
Osborn's four basic rules
what kind of problem you should attack
who to invite
how to write the invitation
when and where to hold your brainstorm

KEEP 'EM ROLLING   87

how you can learn to be a good brainstorm chairman
the list of outlawed killer phrases
one of apologetic phrases
what the secretary does

CONTENTS

how to catch ideas
tricks to keep ideas coming
what you can do about that terrible long silence

AFTER THE STORM IS OVER   105

what you do after the brainstorm
how you can collect extra ideas
what to do with your ideas
who applies judgment
the screened list

IDEAS? IN MY COMPANY?   115

how to sell brainstorming to your boss
the best way to sell a superior
how you can sell new ideas in your company
the strategy and tactics you can use to turn your ideas into action

THE PREACHING PRACTICED   123

actual case histories of brainstorm sessions
the invitation
the line-up
the brainstorm itself
the list of ideas
cold cash results

SOLOS AND SMALL COMBOS   153

how you can brainstorm by yourself
what equipment you need
when and where to solo brainstorm
how to stimulate your subconscious
how to ignite a solo chain reaction
problems for the solo brainstorm
how small groups brainstorm
the quick, on-the-spot brainstorm
what one company has done
variations on a theme

IT COMES KING SIZE, TOO   165

why members of large groups don't contribute ideas
how you can make each member a brainstormer
how you can collect ideas from hundreds of people
sparking a conference or convention
uses of the mass brainstorm
a test case

TAKE IT HOME TO MAMA   177

how you can brainstorm at home

a housewife uses brainstorming
the family brainstorm
problems for the breakfast-table brainstorm
how to make your home life richer with brainstorming

THE SHOE FITS, PUT IT ON   187

how brainstorming fits your business
examples of brainstorming used in many fields
a department-store case history of how it adapted brainstorming to special problems
how brainstorming can work in laboratories and lodges, union meetings, and executive suites, on the campus and the production line, in hospitals and civic organizations
a church case history
and one for travelers

TROUBLES ARE A BRAINSTORMER'S BEST FRIEND   207

how you can turn your problems into advantages
profits from frustration
turning temper into cash
the nose for needs
a company which thrives on problems
how you can find problems
case histories of companies which turned problems into profits
how you can do the same

THE COMPLEAT BRAINSTORMER 227

how to look at your world creatively
how you can invite brainstorms
ways you can solve your problems creatively
how you can make a check list
how you can make an idea bank and an idea museum
your own idea trap

SECRETS OF A SUCCESSFUL IDEA MAN 243

why you should give ideas away
how to exercise your subconscious
the importance of having a deadline
why keep score on yourself
how to make your own wish book
what more ideas would mean to you
the basic secret of all idea men

AMERICA'S LAST FRONTIER 255

one man's creative adventure
what you can do with your own ideas
the most important revolution of our age
what it can mean to your future
how you can be a pioneer in creativity, our last frontier

FOREWORD

I can think of no finer way to enrich a person's life than to stimulate him to a greater use of his creative talents. The ability to be creative—in which the techniques of "brainstorming" play such an important part—is largely a state of mind. It is a state of mind that we all can cultivate.

As a business manager, I have been especially interested in stimulating ideas for two reasons: to benefit the business itself and to help the people who work in that business. In our organization we have had quite a bit of experience with this subject. And I can say that these techniques not only work on specific problems. They also help to broaden a person's outlook on life—to open his whole personality to the "idea concept" and to encourage a constant, fresh eagerness about all the problems of daily living.

Although my comments are being made from a businessman's point of view, I think it is evident that they apply quite generally to all people. Any company or organization that makes and sells products in competition will prosper only as it develops new ideas. This is basic to growth and improvement. To fulfill this objective, the organization must have creative people on all its important areas, such as engineering, manufacturing, sales, and personnel. And it must have good management in seeing that the best results are obtained from those creative people in all those areas.

Yet, whether one's business is large or small, there are some dilemmas in which the manager finds himself. For instance, a very small business, desiring to grow, may find the problem of developing new ideas a difficult and expensive one. Therefore, the need to avoid the failure of working on the wrong idea is vital.

The manager of a large organization is also in a difficult spot. To him, spending money on a poor idea is not so serious because his resources are larger. However, because of this, there is less appreciation of the cost of development. Consequently the controls that he must employ can create an atmosphere that hampers idea men and their productiveness. Thus there are the dual problems of creativity and good management.

Creative ability is most frequently the opposite of good judgment. Creative ability includes the tendency to experiment with novel ideas that might be unsound. It includes a good deal of the gambler's spirit where the individual "sticks his neck out" and tries something new, perhaps even "wild" or "crazy." Therefore, by its very nature, creative ability is on the opposite end of the scale from good judgment.

In other words, if we were to draw a line to represent the various degrees of creative ability and sound judgment, we would put great creativity at one end and sound judgment at the other. The better manager, when rated along this line, would be much closer to the good judgment end than to the creativity end. So we immediately see that a "good manager" may automatically constitute a barrier to an atmosphere that fosters creativity. Consequently, this is a real challenge to business leaders: how to combine a flow of creative new ideas with sound evaluation.

Yet I feel that it is absolutely necessary to cultivate the "idea atmosphere" if an organization is to forge ahead day after day. Business, just as art, needs a climate of open-mindedness—and should not be wary of non-conformists or men who continually pose ideas that run contrary to our orthodox thinking.

When a person is faced with a problem, it seems natural to fall back upon previous experience for answers. In most cases, judgment dictates what is most practical or what has worked in the past. This judgment is the end result of training, which has been instilled in the individual throughout most of his life. From the time the child is old enough to comprehend, he is taught to do what is "best" for himself and for others. He is trained to do the "right" thing. This, then, is the beginning of judgment. This process continues throughout his growth to maturity.

What happens during this period when judgment is developing? What was there before judgment developed? Let's look at a young child. One is immediately struck by his power of imagination. Everything is "real" to him. Everything is alive. The stick he picks up and aims is a gun. The tree he climbs is a mountain or a ship's lookout platform.

Imagination is tolerated in a child but not always encouraged. As he grows older, he is impressed with the fact that his imagination, while a source of amusement, is often not practical. Thus we see that judgment may take the place of imagination completely—or that imagination will be used less and less as judgment is used more and more.

Theoretically, this could lead to a person's having all judgment and no imagination—and don't we seem to run into those persons? Don't some people seem to rely entirely on precedent and experience and seem afraid to try a new slant?

But must judgment be developed at the expense of imagination? I think not. Moreover, I believe we have had experience that proves that ideas can be stimulated and that a climate can be developed, and maintained, in which ideas—as well as good judgment—flourish. We have drawn freely on all sources of research and information and have reached these conclusions, for example, as to what a creative person is.

In the first place, he has a *sensitivity* to problems. Then he also has a *fluency* with ideas in that he thinks of a lot of approaches to a problem. Many of these ideas are characterized by *novelty*. His ideas are new and perhaps different.

The creative man is *flexible*, able to drop one line of thinking and easily take up another one. Also, he has a quality that has been described as *constructive discontent,* a certain restlessness of mind, searching for new and better ways of doing things.

This characteristic has been forcefully described by Harlow H. Curtice, president of General Motors, as "the inquiring mind." It is this attitude, he points out, that "is never satisfied with things as they are . . . is always seeking ways to make things better and do things better." And it is this kind of person who "assumes that everything and anything can be improved."

Now let me describe our experience a bit more—for it is pertinent to this book. When the author, Charles Clark, asked me to write this, I readily agreed. For "creativity" and "brainstorming" have become a real part of the way we operate our business.

For many years, of course, we have had our share of meetings and conferences. In those, we have always tried to develop new and better ways to operate, cut costs, create new products, and improve human relations. But in 1953 we decided to see whether we could do more about creativity—in a scientific, systematic manner. We assembled a group of experts in the field, psychologists and educators. Some said we could determine and develop creativity. Others said this was doubtful. But we decided it should be tried and probably could be done.

From that start we developed a testing program that has been proved psychologically. It is a test that shows how creative a person is, within fairly close limits. This test has been given to more than one thousand people in our own plants and to probably another two thousand outside our organization—folks who borrowed our test to try for themselves.

Then we also began to develop a training program to see whether we could stimulate more ideas in our people . . . ideas for new products, new ways of making those products . . . ideas on anything that might help our whole team. More than one thousand of our people have taken this creativity training, and we know it produces good results. Brainstorming is an important part of this course.

We started out by trying the course on our top executives. They were convinced it could stimulate people into thinking up ideas that would help the entire division. From them we went on to give the course to our engineering people and then to manufacturing supervision.

Everybody seems to like the creativity work. It is, in fact, the most popular of all our educational activities. We have "discovered" that folks like to give their imaginations a workout and, once they know ideas are welcome, they will come up with many good suggestions.

I am proud of the fact that for the past several years our division of General Motors has been a leader in the GM Suggestion Plan. This record stems, at least in part, I feel, from the "climate," the idea-atmosphere, that pervades our organization. That, I believe, is the most important single result to come from our continuing creativity program.

Surely we teach people some specific ways to generate ideas. The techniques described by Charles Clark in this book are followed, and I might say I've even learned some new ones from him. But, above all, we have tried to create a definite feeling among our people, especially our management and technical groups, that our division has a "wide-open mind." I don't believe anybody feels he will be criticized for suggesting something new, untried, or different, even if it might seem "screwball."

So I am delighted to have the honor of suggesting to you that this book will make life a bit better for you and for all who are affected by your life and occupation. At work, at home, in groups or alone, "brainstorming" is fun and is valuable.

Maybe we are highlighting the word "brainstorming" with unusual force. The main idea to get from a book such as this, however, is that the human brain is a wonderful, fantastic, unbelievable instrument—and one that we can use constantly for the betterment of mankind!

Joseph A. Anderson
General Manager
AC Spark Plug Division
of General Motors,
Flint, Mich.

THE DIFFERENCE AN IDEA MAKES

*how ideas make
a difference*

*how ideas can change
your life*

*ideas which have made
a difference
in our world*

*importance of ideas
to the individual,
the company,
community,
and nation*

You know the difference an idea makes.

You may not realize it, but if you look about you where you work, in a large office, on an assembly line, in the government, on a salesman's beat, in a small store, in a laboratory, in the shipping room or the executive suite, you will see the difference an idea makes.

You will see the difference in the men who move ahead. You will see it in the products which make sales records. You will see it in the business which prospers. You will see it in profit and loss statements, on the stock exchange, in the delicatessen which closes, in the headlines. You will see it in your home and other homes, in the family which does things, in your church and lodge, in your political party, in your government. The one quality which turns the ordinary into the extraordinary is ideas.

For example, visit the engineering department of a large manufacturing company, say in the field of electronics, and you will see row upon row of drawing boards and row upon row of engineers, all in shirt sleeves, who look remarkably alike. And they have much in common. Each man in the room has an engineering degree, each has been graduated from the company training program. Most of the men are married, have about the same number of children and the same number of bedrooms in their split-level homes, about fourteen payments left on the car, and seventeen years to go on their mortgage. They all get the same pay, give or take a few dollars.

If you came back in a year to that vast room full of seemingly identical engineers you would see that a strange process had taken place. One man way back on the left had moved his slide rule and drawing pens up to a drawing board at the front of the room. Another came in one day and sat down at a desk, not a drawing board, in an office down the corridor. Still another, apparently lost in the center of the room full of shirt-sleeved workers, moved out to the front office and started to wear a suit jacket and carry a brown leather dispatch case to work instead of a lunch box.

This process might seem strange, mysterious, and completely nonunderstandable viewed from a distance. You might feel like an anthropologist on a South Sea island viewing some native rites that were unaccountable. But if you investigated you would find an enormous difference between the look-alike men in the look-alike shirts in the hangar-sized workroom: the men who moved ahead had ideas.

Sure, not all the ideas were good ones, not all of them worked, others were too expensive, still others had been tried before. But they were ideas, that ingenious, creative element which makes all the difference in our lives.

Notice I said they had ideas, not an idea, and they expressed those ideas. Actually they had a flood of ideas, and, in effect, the whole engineering department depended on the creative energies of a tiny minority.

That fellow on the left was working over a drawing when he had an idea for a new material which would make a better part, at less cost. The next day he worked on another part and realized that one of the manufacturing processes could be eliminated by a redesign. A fortnight later he saw how the company could save money by purchasing stock screws rather than tooling their own connections. All year long he kept seeing the same products and processes as the rest of the men in the room, but in them he saw problems, and then he thought up solutions to those problems.

That man in the middle of the room lost a blueprint one day, and he figured out a coding system so plans couldn't be misplaced so easily. He had a headache and suggested better lights over the drawing boards. Loaded down with work, he devised a new method of drawing designs; trying to arrange his own vacation, he came up with a better vacation schedule. During the year his pet peeves, irritations, frustrations led to new ideas.

That fellow way back in the room went shopping with his wife one evening and sent in ideas on new markets for products the next morning. He met an amateur radio bug and realized how a tube his company manufactured could be adapted for ham radio use. He saw his wife make a ready-mix cake and had an idea for plastic packaging. Building a model plane with his son, he saw how one of the company's oldest products could have a new use in guided missiles. Everything he did set off a chain reaction which resulted in ideas.

As the ideas from the three men came in to their bosses and filtered up through the company, these men became known for their ideas. They were known as idea men, men who cared about the job, men who were thinking all the time, men you could give tough problems to and expect results. When new jobs opened up, departments expanded, their selection was natural. Ideas set them apart from the hundreds of men who had the same advantages and disadvantages they did; ideas made the difference in their careers.

Their ideas also made the difference between the company and its competitors; it swung the balance from loss to profit, from failure to success. Some of the ideas also made the difference in the defense of the free world. For example, the Air Force needed a new radar unit for a supersonic interceptor. One of the engineers had suggested a simple product which could be easily mass-produced. Because of his idea, their bid was by far the lowest. They got the job, made a handsome profit, but most important, the planes got the part in a hurry.

In the same way that engineers look alike, so do companies. They have huge, low plants, large parking lots, carpeted executive suites, sexy receptionists, engineers who need haircuts, sales managers who need to diet, and comptrollers who need to smile. The companies aren't the same, however, and the successful ones have ideas that make the difference.

To understand the full force of ideas, you have to turn to history, but certainly not ancient history. One day in 1915 one man far down the executive ladder wrote a memo and passed it along to his boss. The man with an idea was the assistant traffic manager of the Marconi Wireless Telegraph Company. Here is his memo, which I quote in full because it is one of the most astounding documents in business history:

> *I have in mind a plan of development which would make radio a "household utility" in the same sense as*

the piano or phonograph. The idea is to bring music into the house by wireless.

While this has been tried in the past by wires, it has been a failure because wires do not lend themselves to this scheme. With radio, however, it would seem to be entirely feasible. For example—a radio telephone transmitter having a range of say 25 to 50 miles can be installed at a fixed point where instrumental or vocal music or both are produced. The problem of transmitting music has already been solved in principle, and therefore all the receivers attuned to the transmitting wave length should be capable of receiving such music. The receiver can be designed in the form of a simple "Radio Music Box" and arranged for several different wave lengths, which should be changeable with the throwing of a single switch or pressing of a single button.

The "Radio Music Box" can be supplied with amplifying tubes and a loud-speaking telephone, all of which can be neatly mounted in one box. The box can be placed on a table in the parlor or living room, the switch set accordingly, and the transmitted music received. There should be no difficulty in receiving music perfectly when transmitted within a radius of 25 to 50 miles. Within such a radius there reside hundreds of thousands of families; and as all can simultaneously receive from a single transmitter, there would be no question of obtaining sufficiently loud signals to make the performance enjoyable. . . . The power of the transmitter can be made 5 kw if necessary, to cover even a short radius of 25 to 50 miles; thereby giving extra loud signals in the home if desired. The use of head telephones would be obviated by this method. The development of a small loop antenna to go with each "Radio Music Box" would likewise solve the antennae problem.

The same principle can be extended to numerous other fields—as for example—receiving lectures at home which can be made perfectly audible; also events of national importance can be simultaneously announced and received. Baseball scores can be transmitted in the air by the use of one set installed at the Polo Grounds. The same would be true of other cities. This proposition would be especially interesting to farmers and others living in outlying districts removed from cities. By the purchase of a "Radio Music Box" they could enjoy concerts, lectures, music, recitals, etc., which may be going on in the nearest city within their radius. While I have indicated a few of the most probable fields of usefulness for such a device, yet there are numerous other fields to which the principle can be extended. . . .

In connection with this idea I have had in mind for some time the possibility of connecting up the Wireless Age with the plan, thereby making the Wireless Press a profitable venture. What I have in mind is this:

Every purchaser of a "Radio Music Box" would be encouraged to become a subscriber of the Wireless Age, which would announce in its columns an advance monthly schedule of all lectures, music recitals, etc., to be given in the various cities of the country. With this arrangement the owner of the "Radio Music Box" can learn from the columns of the Wireless Age what is going on in the air at any given time and throw the "Radio Music Box" switch to the point (wave length) corresponding with the music or lecture desired to be heard.

If this plan is carried out, the volume of paid adver-

tising that can be obtained for the Wireless Age on the basis of such proposed increased circulation would in itself be a profitable venture. In other words, the Wireless Age would perform the same mission as is now being performed by the various motion picture magazines which enjoy so wide a circulation.

The manufacture of the "Radio Music Box" including antenna, in large quantities, would make possible their sale at a moderate figure of perhaps $75 per outfit. The main revenue to be derived will be from the sale of "Radio Music Boxes" which, if manufactured in quantities of one hundred thousand or so, could yield a handsome profit when sold at the price mentioned above. Secondary sources of revenue would be from the sale of transmitters and from increased advertising and circulation of the Wireless Age. The Company would have to undertake the arrangements, I am sure, for music recitals, lectures, etc., which arrangements can be satisfactorily worked out. It is not possible to estimate the total amount of business obtainable with this plan until it has been developed and actually tried out, but there are about 15,000,000 families in the United States alone and if only one million or 7% of the total families thought well of the idea, it would, at the figure mentioned, mean a gross business of about $75,000,000, which should yield considerable revenue.

Aside from the profit to be derived from this proposition the possibilities for advertising for the Company are tremendous; for its name would ultimately be brought into the household and wireless would receive national and universal attention.

Like most good ideas, it seems obvious—after it has become

history. Yet we have to remember that in 1915 there was no broadcasting industry. Telegraphy was used for communication, not entertainment. It was a serious business. The memo was tossed aside with a laugh.

For an astonishing five years nothing happened. Then the Radio Corporation of America was formed. The idea man pulled his memo out of his files and sent it along to Owen D. Young, Chairman of the Board of the new company. That was on January 30. On March 3 the idea man was asked by E. W. Rice, Jr., president of RCA, for an estimate of future radio business. The following additional memo was written:

The "Radio Music Box" proposition (regarding which I reported to Mr. Nally in 1915 and to Mr. Owen D. Young on January 31, 1920) required considerable experimentation and development; but, having given the matter much thought, I feel confident in expressing the opinion that the problems involved can be met. With reasonable speed in design and development, a commercial product can be placed on the market within a year or so.

Should this plan materialize it would seem reasonable to expect sales of one million (1,000,000) "Radio Music Boxes" within a period of three years. Roughly estimating the selling price at $75 per set, $75,000,000 can be expected. This may be divided approximately as follows:

1st Yr.—100,000 Radio Music Boxes	$ 7,500,000
2nd Yr.—300,000 Radio Music Boxes	22,500,000
3rd Yr.—600,000 Radio Music Boxes	45,000,000
Total	$75,000,000

By now you should have guessed the name of the idea

man. Today he is world-famous as General David Sarnoff, Chairman of the Board of the Radio Corporation of America.

To finish the story of this amazing memo, compare his estimates with the actual figures of the first three years "Radio Music Boxes" were sold by RCA:

1922	$11,000,000
1923	$22,500,000
1924	$50,000,000
Total	$83,500,000

Here was an idea that turned an assistant traffic manager into one of the most influential and wealthy men in the United States and formed the basis of a new industry which has affected every one of us. The way we act, the way we think, the way we talk, every nook and cranny of our world, private and public, has been changed by David Sarnoff's idea and its direct descendant, television.

The magic that ignited this revolution was a simple, powerful idea and a man who had both the drive to write it down and the stubbornness to keep pushing it for the five years when he was ridiculed.

Each one of us should understand that there is always resistance to new ideas and not be discouraged into paralysis by it. Such inertia is natural and normal.

For example, take the zipper. In 1926 a cub advertising salesman called on the Hookless Fastener Company, known today as Talon, in Meadville, Pennsylvania.

"Art," someone asked him, "how can we sell more of our zippers?"

Art thought a moment. "I've got an idea. Why not sell

them to men's clothing manufacturers to put them on flies instead of buttons?"

They roared. They'd never heard anything so ridiculous. The arguments against the idea came up, the killer phrases: "That's silly." "Men won't wear them." "We'll run into trouble." "There will be accidents." "We'll be sued."

It took four years before they accepted the idea, which today provides a huge share of their profits.

Behind each industry is a man with an idea. Before World War I a businessman-naturalist hunting fine fox furs in Labrador noticed that fish and game frozen in blasts of midwinter wind forty to fifty degrees below zero were more flavorful than foods frozen in spring and fall. He wondered why. To find out he cut paper-thin slices of fish and found that the quick-frozen flesh was firm, but that the slower-frozen fish were grainy with large ice crystals and leaked juice when they thawed.

Several years later he happened into the wholesale fish business. "I felt Americans would eat more fish if it could be kept really fresh during shipment," he wrote years later in the *Reader's Digest*. "I borrowed the corner of an ice-cream plant in New Jersey and started experiments in mechanical freezing. In 1923 I organized a company and the next year put quick-frozen fish on the market. Soon we went broke. But my wife and I hocked our insurance and used the money to design an automatic freezer and form a new company. Eventually I got the backing of several wealthy men. In 1929 we sold out our frozen foods business for $22,000,000."

His name, of course, was Clarence Birdseye. And what a difference his idea is still making in every home today. It has created thousands upon thousands of jobs: people who make freezers and service them, people who raise food for freezing companies, people who pack and sell frozen foods, and people who eat them all year round. His idea has revolutionized one of the nation's basic industries.

One thing we should realize, however, is the importance of small ideas and rearrangements of what we already know. Those ideas have their place just as much as the great revolutionary ideas.

George J. Abrams, vice-president in charge of advertising for Revlon, points out the importance of all sorts of ideas in the competitive business world. He mentions the idea of the aerosol container which was used first with whipped cream and later shaving cream. He tells how a small company like Breck in Springfield, Massachusetts, successfully competes with huge international firms in the creative warfare of business because of good ideas. Breck doesn't have a million-dollar TV program; it does have beauty parlors across the nation using and recommending its product because of brilliant merchandising ideas.

In almost every case of profit-making products there is a good idea behind the product. Abrams cites a competitive product which became the largest selling deodorant on the market. Why? Because it rolls on, using the principle of a ball-point pen—an idea which created millions upon millions of dollars of business a decade ago. His own company, Revlon, has a long record of successful ideas. One is Love Pat. For generations women have been putting loose, messy powder into expensive compacts. Revlon pressed powder, under high pressure, into inexpensive but attractive plastic compacts any woman could afford. Overnight the Love Pat compact became the largest-selling item in the face-powder field. "I know of no business weapon so powerful as a strong idea," concludes Abrams.

There's Herbert Piker, a young Hamilton, Ohio, manufacturer, who sat staring at a minnow bucket. He had inherited a metal box company, which was in bad shape. He didn't know which way to turn. But as he stared he thought, "Why not put a layer of insulation between those two cans?" That was the beginning of the Scotch Cooler. In four years his rundown business was grossing more than five million dollars annually.

The profit from a good idea is easy to figure out, but J. A. Anderson of the AC Spark Plug Division of General Motors has pointed out the other side of the coin. "We have the costs of ideas not thought up," he has said. "That is a very definite cost. We have the costs of ideas thought of too late. We have the costs of ideas not developed to their fullest potential. We have the costs of ideas not thought of at all."

Ideas which people have had—or not had—have made the difference in the whole history of man—simple ideas and complex ideas, little ideas and big ideas. What unknown genius first discovered the wheel? Who was the person—was it a woman—who discovered wheat could be made into bread? Our whole world is defined by the men who had the ideas that made possible the automobile, the bridge, the skyscraper, the airplane, the ocean liner, the telephone, the light which turns night into day. Who can estimate the value of the idea of a curved ax handle which made it possible for one man to clear more wilderness and create a new world?

What price can be put on the idea of freedom that made children defy Russian tanks in Hungary in 1956?

The essential difference between nations is ideas; the Free World will stand or fall on the strength of our ideas. In a Hell Bomb age ideas are still more powerful than any other force known to man.

THE STORK DOESN'T BRING THEM

*how you give birth
to ideas*

*how the subconscious
works*

*a test to show how
your subconscious
creates ideas*

*the practical results
of impractical ideas*

*how creative people
have harnessed
their subconscious*

*how you can do
the same*

Every husband has had this experience. He's talking to his wife about the five-spade bid, doubled, redoubled, and vulnerable that they made the night before, when she says suddenly, "They should be green, don't you think so?"

"What?" he answers, husbandlike.

"They should be green, sort of a yellowish green with a touch of blue," she says in tones reserved for a rather stupid child.

"What should be green-blue with a touch of yellow?" he roars in tones reserved for a husband whose wife has just talked to him as if he were a rather stupid child.

"Why, the drapes, silly."

"What drapes?" he repeats.

"The new drapes in the living room we'll need if we get that sofa like the Eshbaughs'."

"What sofa like the Eshbaughs'?" "We were playing bridge at the Gunthers', and Jim led from his ace, and you . . ."

If the marriage is young, the conversation will go on and on as the puzzled husband tries to understand his wife's thought processes. She will explain that she had been talking about the hand when she thought of the dress Jeannie was wearing, and how it clashed with the Eshbaughs' sofa at the luncheon a week before, and that gave her the idea for just the right drapes to go with the sofa.

If her husband groans in anguish, she'll smile and say, "Why, dear, it's perfectly logical." It isn't, of course, and her husband will nod knowingly and comment more than a trifle smugly about "a woman's mind."

What he doesn't realize is that he has the same kind of mind, and if he wants to get ahead in his logical, masculine world of business, he'd better start to use it.

What had solved his wife's drapery problem was her subconscious mind, which went on working during a week in which she kept house, cooked, drove her husband to the train, attended church, slept, played bridge, ran a PTA meeting. The same illogical mind can solve the problems of mortgage debt, investment, administrative reorganization and industrial design, if it is allowed to do the job.

Many men won't let it work for them, however. They are afraid of their subconscious. Some feel, like our husband, that the subconscious is somehow unmanly, a woman's mind. Others feel it is frivolous, not at all gray flannel enough for their business. Still others believe it is a will-of-the-wisp thing that can't be trusted, that it will somehow betray them, and that it most certainly can't be trained to work in the everyday business world.

They are woefully wrong. Most businesses and professions are guided by the landmarks erected by men who have made brilliant use of their creative minds.

Harley J. Earl, styling chief of General Motors, once said, "If a particular group appears to be bogging down over a new fender or grille or interior trim, I sometimes wander into their quarters, make some irrelevant or even zany observation, and then leave. It is surprising what effect a bit of peculiar behavior will have. First-class minds will seize on anything out of the ordinary and race off, looking for explanations and hidden meanings. That's all I want them to do —start exercising their imaginations. The ideas will soon pop up."

The subconscious mind isn't a logical creature which proceeds from point one to point two to point three in a straight line. It's an illogical character who skips from point one to point eight to point three to point seven, trying all sorts of unusual combinations, making use of every observation and stimulus to create new solutions.

This is its importance. It is creative. The ideas that make a difference are the product of our creative minds.

Take this test and find out how your own creative mind works. In three minutes see how many objects you can sketch which have a circle as a main element in their design. Just use a few lines on the circles on page 42 to identify your ideas, which might start: wheel, tire, steering wheel, and so on.

Notice how your mind leaps from category to category. For example, your test might run wheel, tire, steering wheel, then hop into another category—speedometer, watch, clock, and then to still another—doughnut, cruller, cooky, pizza; then make another leap to plate, saucer, and so on.

If our minds worked logically we would exhaust every category and list hundreds of types of wheels before we moved on to gears, and list a thousand gears. Instead, our minds bound forward. In a small way this illustrates the leaps which have measured man's progress.

One European scientist made a study of his fellow workers and found that 75 per cent had made their most important discoveries when away from the job. The history of scientific progress is studded with cases which back him up.

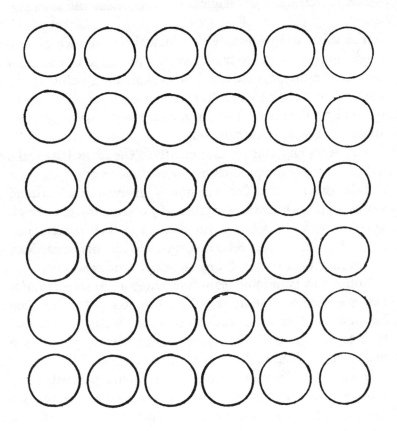

For example, in 1920 a Canadian surgeon, Frederick Grant Banting, worked all day long on a lecture on diabetes. The more he read about the disease the more confused he became. At last he gave up and staggered to bed.

Then in early hours of the morning he suddenly sat up, turned on a light and wrote: "Tie off pancreatic duct of dogs. Wait six to eight weeks for degeneration. Remove residue and extract." That idea, shot forth by his subconscious in the middle of the night, led directly to the discovery of insulin.

Every profession and every industry has many such cases. One day in 1895 a man in Brookline, Massachusetts, found his razor dull. Let King C. Gillette tell what happened: "It was not only dull, but it was beyond the point of successful stropping and it needed honing, for which it must be taken to a barber or to a cutler. As I stood there with the razor in my hand, my eyes resting on it lightly as a bird settling down on its nest—the Gillette razor was born. I saw it all in a moment, and in that same moment many unvoiced questions were asked and answered more with the rapidity of a dream than by the slow process of reasoning.

"A razor is only a sharp edge and all back of that edge is but a support for that edge," he thought. "Why do they spend so much material and time in fashioning a backing which has nothing to do with shaving? Why do they forge a great piece of steel and spend so much labor in hollow-grinding it when they could get the same result by putting an edge on a piece of steel that was only thick enough to hold an edge?"

His mind charged ahead. "At that time and in that moment it seemed as though I could see the way the blade could be held in a holder; then came the idea of sharpening the two opposite edges on the tiny piece of steel that was in uniform thickness throughout, thus doubling its service; and following in sequence came the clamping plates for the blade with a handle equally disposed between the two edges of the blade. All this came more in pictures than in thought," he remembered, "as though the razor were already a finished thing and held before my eyes. I stood there before that mirror in a trance of joy at what I saw. Fool that I was, I knew little about razors and practically nothing about steel, and could not foresee the trials and tribulations that I was to pass through before the razor was a success. But I believed in it, and joyed in it. I wrote to my wife, who was visiting in Ohio, 'I have got it; our fortune is made.'"

The fact he knew nothing about steel or about razors carries an important lesson to all. Gillette had to learn about them before his razor was a success. In fact for six years, yes, six full years, his razor was a joke to his friends, but eventually it made industrial history. If he had known anything about the business, however, his judicial mind might have convinced him he was crazy before he saw the whole picture, and it might have even erased it all from his memory.

Most important was the fact that his mind was open to see the vision. We have to be ready to receive ideas that our subconscious is waiting to give us, and then apply stern judgment in evaluating them.

The vision can come at any time, and many wise idea men always stand ready for the lightning to strike. Lewis Strauss, Chairman of the Atomic Energy Commission, always has a memo pad at his side when he retires. He'll often have an idea and scrawl it down in the dark, then stuff the note in his slipper so he'll remember it in the morning. United Automobile Workers' president Walter Reuther has his lieutenant imitate his habit of incessantly making notes during conversations, meetings, negotiations, lunches. Samuel Leibowitz, the great trial lawyer, has said he's won a hundred cases lying in bed. He always kept a notebook and a pencil on a bedside table.

John Foster Dulles has a scratch pad handy on all his travels. Ralph Reed, head of American Express, seldom goes to bed before 2 A.M., but he still frequently wakes up in the night to scratch down important ideas on a pad beside his bed. The author Thomas Costain lies abed in the morning purposely to let his mind wander idly over the writing ahead. When he sits down at his typewriter he finds many of his problems already solved for him. Many authors stop writing just before they have run out of steam, and let their subconscious mind carry the story forward as they walk, read, sleep, and eat.

This can operate for anyone, contractor as well as novelist, laborer as well as executive. Ray A. Hammerstrom, a fifty-seven-year-old steel worker for Jones and Loughlin, took a nap one day and had a dream about a switch for the rolling mills. Eleven previous switches had failed to do the job. His dream solved the problem and earned him a check for fifteen thousand dollars from his grateful employers.

John Fox, president of Minute Maid frozen foods, often tells a story of his early days as an IBM salesman when he sold a company automatic machines that didn't seem to fit into that particular accounting problem.

"Finally, near the end of my rope," he remembers, "and

quite seriously wondering if I would be fired when Wamsutta learned the truth and the machines were sent back, I spent one whole evening at the New Bedford Hotel recapitulating and reviewing the elements of the problem. With no glimmer of an answer, I went to bed, exhausted and completely discouraged.

"The next morning as I was sitting in the bathtub," he goes on, "the answers to my problem started to come to me as clearly as if they were being written on the tile wall around the tub. I jumped out and, without bothering to dry myself, hastily wrote down the procedure that had seemingly just popped into my mind."

The subconscious is like that, and we are wise if we give it a chance to do its job. Thoreau has said, "A really efficient laborer will be found not to crowd his day with work."

Some executives follow his advice by putting letters which are difficult to answer on the bottom of the pile. When they are dictating answers to the other letters on top, they discover they have unconsciously, or actually subconsciously, solved the problem. When they come to the unanswerable letters they have the answer on the tip of their tongue. Raymond Loewy keeps a number of projects going at once. When he's stuck, he moves on to a new piece of work and lets his subconscious keep plugging away at the old one.

All those people know that although the subconscious may seem to be flitting from one subject to another, dabbling in this, starting that, dropping it, running off to something else, it's not gold-bricking but doing its job.

The subconscious uses every scrap of information that comes its way. Solid statistics, basic principles learned in graduate school, authoritative articles read and re-read, the fruit of long years of formal experience and logical study, all are grist for the mill. It also works with fragments of sentences seen on the back of someone else's paper in the subway, a flash of unusual color on a rainy night, a memory of an attic on a rainy afternoon gone before, a phrase overheard at a cocktail party, the shape of a bee's wing, the sound of a baby's cry.

Every ingredient of life is used in the wonderful laboratory of the creative mind. It is anything but a lazy place. The subconscious never rests. It is constantly trying to fit things together, to see life in a new way, to solve unsolvable problems. Its powers are enormous.

Recently a technique has been developed which executives, scientists, housewives, people in every area of life, alone or in groups, can use to tap that tremendous source of power.

This revolutionary technique of idea production, tested and practiced in hundreds of offices, plants, and laboratories across the country, is called brainstorming.

BRAINSTORMING? WHAT'S THAT?

history of brainstorming

*problems of old-
style conferences*

*how brainstorming
can solve
many of them*

*how you can
brainstorm*

*some cash results
of brainstorming*

*leading organizations
which are using
brainstorming*

*reasons individuals
and groups
should both use
brainstorming*

When Dr. James B. Conant was president of Harvard University he not only made many revolutionary changes in the policies, administration and curriculum of many of its schools; he also became a leading force in U.S. education, a constant source of new and stimulating ideas. It is significant that during his years at Harvard he kept a picture of a turtle on the wall of his office with the caption: "Behold the turtle. He makes progress only when his neck is out."

This is the basic reason for brainstorming, dramatically expressed. It is a technique which encourages people to stick their necks out so that radically new ideas will constantly be produced.

When was the last time you heard anyone come up with a radically new and unconventional idea in an old-style conference or committee meeting? I can't remember one. Conferences are supposed to stimulate thought, but, as we all know, they usually stifle it.

You know the saying, "A camel is an animal which looks like it was made by a committee." Committee meetings in almost every case are the place for compromise, diplomacy, or careful one-upmanship. The members spend ten minutes analyzing the problem, fifty minutes arguing about it.

There are good reasons why the conference or committee usually breaks down. Generally the man running it is the boss. He knows it, and you know it. He is judging you. Your promotion, pay raise, or even your security depends in part on the showing you make in conference. One doesn't dare to do anything daring, does one? At least, not unless it is well calculated. Spontaneity is decidedly not cricket. Yet spontaneous ideas are usually the ones which make a difference.

Then there is nothing democratic about committee meetings. Ideas can't be discussed openly in a dictatorship. In the usual conference the ideas of the boss carry more weight than anyone else. He has his prejudices, and his preferences are well known. It's easy to step on the toes of other committee members too; to seem to hint that Joe's project is bogging down, or that Pete really should have come up with your idea. It's better to shut up than to start a feud.

Most of us are oh so very civilized in committee, and therefore the meeting deteriorates into a sort of hen session in which everyone praises everyone else while trying to get the knife between his neighbor's ribs, quickly and deeply. First, "That's a real great idea, Joe, you can sure come up with them." And then the lunge, "Remember old zipper shoe promotion?" The company lost $876,000,000 on that one, and good old Joe was responsible.

Then, of course, there are the feuds. Committee members often take to the battle lines ready to take pot shots as soon as anyone has a new idea. If not on principle, then certainly for sport. It's easy to be clever when negative, and after all, if you didn't get money for your spring promotion, why should Pete get his?

There are many more solid reasons why the conference rarely produces new ideas. It is usually called for reasons of judgment or co-ordination. The atmosphere is judicial. Company policy, finances and other such essentially negative matters are of prime concern. Often they should be, but add to this man's natural tendency to turn down ideas, and you get the usual negative conference.

Yet we cannot work alone. Our society is too vast and complex. We must work out many problems in conference if our eight right hands are to know what our eight left hands are doing.

This is the spot Alex Osborn found himself in nineteen years ago when he took over as executive vice president of Batten, Barton, Durstine and Osborn, one of the largest advertising agencies in the world. Conferences were necessary. Conferences were negative. Yet, especially in advertising, new ideas, hundreds upon hundreds of new ideas, were vital. Brainstorming, more or less as it is practiced today, was founded by him as a brilliant counterattack on negative conference thinking. He noticed that every conference he attended was dominated by a "No, no, a thousand times no" atmosphere. Ideas were suffocated if they were mentioned, and too many idea people who knew this remained silent. The conference was dominated by an individual or the ghost of a policy.

Brainstorming is a strategy with which a problem can be attacked—in fact, literally stormed—by dozens of ideas. The attack can be carried on by one person, by two or three, by an Osborn's dozen, or by even hundreds. The important thing is that the most creative portion of the brain, the subconscious, has its full fire directed right at the problem under attack. Ideas—new, different, crazy ideas—are allowed to get to the subconscious and set off the marvelous chain reaction of free association.

Osborn developed a conference technique which BBDO has used with great success, and which has been imitated all over the country. In his idea session a dozen people sit around a table and are given a problem, the more specific the better. Then everyone pops out with any idea which comes into his head. It's a bull session put to work. No judgment is allowed, no negative thoughts. The sky is the limit on ideas. Nobody would laugh at the idea of the radio, the way David Sarnoff's memo was ridiculed. Offbeat approaches, silly solutions, zany notions are the raw material of a brainstorm. Everyone is encouraged to hitch-hike on other people's ideas. Each idea is recorded by a secretary. There is a time limit, and when it is up, the conference is over.

The next day the ideas are copied, and the panel chairman puts the list into categories; later the account executive with the account under discussion evaluates the ideas. Then it is all right to say this is against policy; this costs too much; this can't be done. But by then the person with the power to veto new ideas is faced with a concrete suggestion, and he has to have a real argument against it. Often the ideas are obvious—and good. They are ideas which never would have been mentioned in a normal conference where the members would be afraid to mention them because of ridicule or repercussion.

In the brainstorm session each person is uninhibited. Instead of being penalized by ideas, he is encouraged to have them. In addition he is stimulated by the truly creative thinking of the people around him.

Such brainstorm sessions have become a regular BBDO policy. In 1956 forty-seven continuing brainstorm panels held

401 sessions in which some 34,000 ideas were produced. Experience proved that about 6% of those ideas were worthy of adoption or development. This means a net output of some 2,000 worth-while ideas per year—ideas which otherwise would remain unborn.

BBDO had one brainstorm session for the New Castle folding door concern which wanted to get people to go through model homes and see their doors in action. The agency came up with 154 ideas. New Castle thought they were so good they passed 153 on to their clients. Ever hear of a batter, even a Mickey Mantle, batting .993?

The agency had several regional offices brainstorm names for a combination washer-drier for Easy Washer Corporation, and could not believe the results when they added them up. They had 993 unduplicated names.

BBDO brainstormed 61 ideas to increase long-distance phone calls. Forty-one were on the screened list given to the client; a total of 16 were used.

Brainstorming has proved itself with practical results to such a degree that it is used by banks, colleges, research laboratories, churches, the military services, civic organizations, political parties—in fact, it is an integral part of the operation of eight of the nation's ten largest corporations.

Here is a list of some organizations which are using brainstorming today:

ABBOT LABORATORIES
AIR UNIVERSITY, MAXWELL FIELD
ALUMINUM CORPORATION OF AMERICA
ARMSTRONG CORK
ARMY COMMAND MANAGEMENT SCHOOL

CHAPTER THREE

B. ALTMAN'S DEPARTMENT STORE
BAUER AND BLACK
BETTER HOMES AND GARDENS
BOY SCOUTS OF AMERICA
BRISTOL-MYERS

CAMPBELL SOUPS
CARBORUNDUM COMPANY
CHICAGO TRIBUNE
CHRISTMAS CLUB CORPORATION
CORNING GLASS
CREOLE PETROLEUM CORPORATION
CROWN ZELLERBACH

DE SOTO
DU PONT

EASTERN GAS AND FUEL ASSOCIATES
EASTMAN KODAK
ESSO
ETHYL CORPORATION

FIRESTONE TIRE AND RUBBER

GENERAL ELECTRIC
GENERAL FOODS
GENERAL MOTORS
B. F. GOODRICH
GOODYEAR TIRE AND RUBBER CO.

HARVARD BUSINESS SCHOOL
H. J. HEINZ
HERCULES POWDER
HOTPOINT

ILLINOIS BELL TELEPHONE COMPANY

BRAINSTORMING? WHAT'S THAT?

INTERNATIONAL BUSINESS MACHINES
INTERNATIONAL SALT

KRAFT FOODS

LILY-TULIP CUP

MASSACHUSETTS INSTITUTE OF TECHNOLOGY
MINNESOTA MINING AND MANUFACTURING

NATIONAL CASH REGISTER
NAVAL ORDNANCE LABORATORIES
NEW BRUNSWICK, N.J., PRESBYTERIAN CHURCH
NEW YORK YOUNG REPUBLICAN CLUB
NORTHWESTERN UNIVERSITY

OWENS-ILLINOIS GLASS

PATTERSON, N.J., CHAMBER OF COMMERCE

RCA
REMINGTON ARMS
REMINGTON RAND
REYNOLDS METALS CORPORATION

SEARS ROEBUCK
STANDARD OIL OF CALIFORNIA

TAYLOR INSTRUMENT
TRANS-WORLD AIRLINES

U. S. AIR FORCE ROTC UNITS
U. S. RUBBER
U. S. STEEL
UNIVERSITY OF SOUTHERN CALIFORNIA

Once you accept Alex Osborn's basic fundamental of green-light thinking you will find as many ways to brainstorm as there are brainstorms. This is not a formal ritual, but a new art which can be adapted to almost any problem and any situation. It is used by technical people to pioneer in an engineering field. It is used by conservative corporations to encourage new ideas in an inhibiting atmosphere. It is used by families to decide where to go on a vacation.

The advantages of brainstorming are many, and you will constantly find new ones as you practice it. First, think of the advantages brainstorming gives you as an individual. It arms you with a long list of creative ways, new and vigorous, to solve your old problems. There is no way to overestimate the importance of this personal idea inventory.

Progress is marked by the way in which we overcome problems. The difference between Joe Smith, who stays rooted in one spot, and Bill Jones, who moves on, lies in the fact that Bill is a problem solver. He sees problems and he sees unusual ways to solve them. He is an idea man, a person who is first a thinker, and second a doer. The best way you can develop into an idea man is to brainstorm the problems that confront you. If you do this you will have a flood of new ideas, a whole weapon system with which to attack the problems which face you, your family, your company, your community.

As you look at the lists of new ideas which you have had and as you put those ideas to work, you will become a new man. You will have confidence in yourself as a person who has ideas, an individual who can do and has done the impossible. You will realize that you have creative powers you never knew existed, and by using them you will bring a new dimension and a new force into your life.

This new feeling of accomplishment will spread from you

to the men and women you work with. You will share with other brainstorm members a real feeling of team accomplishment. You will have sparked one another, conquered, if you will, new mountains together. Your group will feel a contagious enthusiasm and satisfaction in having done what had been given up as impossible.

Another important personal benefit from brainstorming is that your creative skill will snowball. As you learn how to suspend judgment and storm old roadblocks with new vigor, you will do it much more effectively. There is an important lesson in this. People used to think that only a small minority could rule. We in America proved that that is not true. But still people think that only a few people can have ideas, that there is a sort of Divine Right of Intellectuals. That is not true, either. The art of having ideas can be taught, developed, and mastered by a great share of our population. This does not mean, of course, that every Tom, Dick, and Harry can have great ideas. What it does mean is that most of us can have ideas of some dimension, ideas which can make our world a better and richer place in which to live. When you practice brainstorming, you will be amazed at the ideas you will have.

Once you start having a flood of ideas, and after you see them going to work to solve problems that have previously been unsolvable, you will start having original ideas in all sorts of situations which have previously been stultifying and unproductive. You will go to committee meetings and conferences, to conversations with your boss or your secretary, to hours of work alone in your office, and you will find new thoughts popping up in old routines. You will become impatient with the old negative decisions, the casual dismissal of unorthodox thoughts. You will be irritated when your company or your associates run away from the real problems or give up without really trying to solve them. Personally, you will be motivated to have new ideas and to put them to work.

And don't forget that last point. When you create a backlog of new, exciting, workable, challenging ideas they demand to be put to work. They are a constant force pushing you on. Problems that might have been solved with your ideas and have been bypassed will be a daily goad to you to try to get them working. Here again brainstorming goes to work. You will brainstorm new ways of turning your ideas into action. You will brainstorm the problem of selling new ideas in your company, and you will come up with workable techniques which will not only sell your ideas, but create an atmosphere in which other good ideas which have been made idle by old prejudices and negative thinking can be put on the job of problem-solving.

You will also find that you will get much more mileage out of your ideas than you ever expect. Say, for example, that you have responsibility for a packaging problem. You may brainstorm, "How to package product X," and come up with 133 ideas. You may use only four or five of the ideas, but now you have an inventory of more than a hundred ideas from which you can easily choose ones to solve problems in packaging products Y and Z. You will find yourself consciously and subconsciously reaching back into this inventory during your daily work, and a year or two later the investment of a thirty-five-minute brainstorm session will still be paying rich dividends.

Most important of all, perhaps, is that each of us too easily accepts what we think is the inevitable. We classify too many of our problems as impossible, or worse still, accept that classification from somebody else. Once we have practiced brainstorming and discovered the magic of new ideas, we will find our horizons retreating far before us. Our old job will become a new adventure, a fresh challenge waiting to respond to the vigor of one person's creative thinking.

Brainstorming, however, has rich results for management as well as for the individual.

Every corporation has a vast natural resource of people who possess new, vital talent. Every company must depend on new ideas, a process of re-examination and re-creation if it is to maintain its status or to improve it in a competitive world. Brainstorming is one way a corporation can cut through the forest of organization to find new talent and encourage it. In every department there are people bogged down in detail, paralyzed by routine, who have the ability within themselves to produce money-making ideas. Usually they do not even know they have this skill, and if they do, often as not they feel they have no way to express it. Inadvertently many a company has placed an "Ideas Not Wanted" sign on each executive door. Brainstorming tears down those signs. It reaches the people who can create. It stimulates them, jogs management, gives expression to the creative human resource within the corporation.

Brainstorming has other advantages to the sprawling corporation. It improves communication between individuals, and therefore between departments and divisions. Since a brainstorm group is made up of people with a wide variety of specialties, who rarely get together, it throws bridges across the usual moats which hamper free and creative communication. These men get to know one another—comptroller and research scientist, salesman and secretary, shipping-room boss and production-line foreman—they work together, learn to trust and appreciate each other and share the excitement of group accomplishment.

Brainstorming is an important way to make necessarily routine jobs more interesting to workers at all levels. It breaks up the killing monotony and forces workers attending a brainstorm session to look at their work in a new light, in fact, to look at themselves and their position in the company with fresh perspective.

Brainstorming sessions are much more effective than wastebasket-bound memos, unread bulletin board messages, ignored editorials in the company paper, to make company problems real to employees. When a problem is presented to them, for example, a problem of economy, not as a do-not-touch blast from the front office, but as a how-can-you-help-us appeal from the very top, the response is often spectacular.

Especially in a time of high salaries, the hours and minutes wasted in a company can mean the difference between success and bankruptcy. Quick blitzkrieg brainstorm sessions will save hours upon hours spent by highly paid people in wasteful, noncreative, old-style conferences, where most of the time is spent in fighting old battles, rephrasing old debates and generally trying to one-up each other, to the general destruction of the company.

As an individual develops an inventory or idea bank from

brainstorm sessions, so does the company. Proper distribution of brainstorm results can give all sorts of people throughout the corporation a backlog of new ways to solve old problems. On that list of 133 packaging ideas, for example, might be ideas which would be used throughout the year to spark a new advertising campaign, to solve a damage problem in shipping, or even to create a new product.

Most important of all, brainstorming develops a company atmosphere in which new ideas are ignited and encouraged. If management formally seeks out new ideas, and if everyone constantly sees their practical value, then ideas will begin to flow in from people who had previously been inhibited. The idea men won't be scorned or laughed at, and even the most apparently screwball ideas will be given a thoughtful hearing. This creative atmosphere is the trademark of a company which is going places.

Of course, the final test of brainstorming is the solid ideas it turns out. Let's look at the record.

Reynolds Metals Company heard that Quaker Oats was considering a new package for Aunt Jemima's Cornbread Mix. Reynolds' packaging salesmen, engineers, and designers sat down to brainstorm the problem. The result is a prize-winning package which is actually an aluminum baking pan. A big brainstorm bonus for Reynolds was the fact that in the session one man thought of the way oleomargarine used to be colored by squeezing it in a plastic bag. He came up with the idea of selling Quaker Oats a way of putting the mix itself in a Reynolds polyethylene bag, to which other ingredients, such as eggs, could be added and mixed. That made a double sale for the company. Then another fellow suggested the cover be an actual photograph of the mixing procedure printed on, you guessed it, Reyseal. Triple profits for Reynolds.

Reynolds isn't the only company which is making a buck from brainstorming. General Motors AC Spark Plug Division came up with more than a hundred ideas on how to finish off a casting. Bristol-Myers has boosted off-season sales with brainstormed ideas; for example, they offered hand lotion during the summer with a sample of their new deodorant, Ban.

Motorola brainstormed the problem of testing radio and TV speakers. One idea that came out of the sessions—making tests by oscilloscope—reduced error, cut space taken up by testing equipment, and saved 25 per cent in salaries paid testers under the old system.

All sorts of brainstorm results have proved extremely effective. Glass Wax had the idea of selling twenty-three Christmas stencils with glass wax so that windows could be decorated with fancy, delicate, lacy snowflakes and other designs. It was a whale of a profitable item.

When floods struck a number of New England transportation companies in October, 1955, the trade magazine *Fleet Owner* had a quick brainstorming session and sent out a mimeographed supplement with hundreds of suggestions on what to do after the flood. Each section—"Tips to save your flood-hit buildings and terminals"; "Tips to save your shop and road equipment"—was printed on one side of one piece of paper so they could be handed to the man in charge of the particular salvage problem.

One retailer brainstormed on ideas on how to sell a chair

covering. He got forty-five ideas, picked the best nine, and "sold out chair fabrics that had not moved for over two years." General Electric, one of the first companies to teach creative thinking on a large scale, recently needed a quick method of joining two electrical conductors together. A brainstorm session produced 175 ideas in thirty minutes.

These stories could be multiplied a hundred times. Brainstorming is being tested every day in the most competitive fields and found to be a profit-making way of getting valuable new ideas.

The final test is you. Try it and see what happens. In the next chapters you will learn how.

MIXING THE WITCH'S BREW

*how you can
set up a classic
brainstorm session*

*Osborn's four
basic rules*

*what kind of
problem you should
attack*

who to invite

*how to write
the invitation*

*when and where
to hold
your brainstorm*

Brainstorming is a husky, lusty young man with lots of drive. He will survive and produce dozens of new ideas under the most adverse conditions. He will break out of the chains of convention, conservatism, and just plain sluggishness. He can spark new ideas in every sort of area, in churches and laboratories, executive suites and machinist shops. He is an extremely hardy young animal. But there is one way to kill him. That is to fit him to a strait jacket.

All of us who practice brainstorming must constantly remember this. Brainstorming is not a cult; it must not have a ritual. There are ways I practice brainstorming that I have found most successful. But they are not the only ways. Other people have entirely different approaches and just as much success. As more people try the technique there will be more ways of practicing it.

After all, brainstorming is a method of creative thinking. It is based on the premise that there are constantly better ways of doing things; new ideas, methods, materials, and ever changing combinations of old ones.

It would be both dangerous and ridiculous if I were to wrap brainstorming in a cocoon of strict rules and regulations. This book will not do that. I will tell you what I have discovered about brainstorming. I will show you how it has worked. But you will have to take it from there.

In the next four chapters I will show in detail how the "classic" brainstorm operates. It has a panel of about a dozen members, give or take two or three. This is an unnecessary restriction. Later in the book I shall reveal brainstorming techniques which I have used successfully with two or three people, with several hundred, and with one man, alone. The one basic ingredient of any brainstorm session is Osborn's four rules: *

1 CRITICISM IS RULED OUT
   Adverse judgment of ideas must be withheld until later.

2 "FREE-WHEELING" IS WELCOMED
   The wilder the idea, the better; it is easier to tame down than to think up.

3 QUANTITY IS WANTED
   The greater the number of ideas, the more the likelihood of winners.

4 COMBINATION AND IMPROVEMENT ARE SOUGHT
   In addition to contributing ideas of their own, participants should suggest how ideas of others can be turned into better ideas; or how two or more ideas can be joined into still another idea.

Brainstorming's growth, however, came from the twelve-man brainstorm panel, and it is still the size most used, since it is ideal for the corporation which must try so hard to break through its natural limitations and get new ideas. We will follow such a conventional brainstorm through each step from invitation to implementation of its ideas, and then we

*From *Applied Imagination, Principles and Procedures of Creative Thinking,* 1957 ed., by Alex F. Osborn, copyright 1953 by Charles Scribner's Sons. Reprinted by permission of the publisher, Charles Scribner's Sons.

will study the case history of actual brainstorm sessions. Remember all the time, however, that only the four basic rules are necessary. You have a mission and a challenge—to use creative thinking to make your own brainstorm session better and more productive than any that have gone before. Just as there is no negative thinking allowed in the brainstorm session, so there won't be in this book.

The secret of a good brainstorming session, like a good proposal of marriage, is spontaneity. And the secret of such spontaneity is, of course, good planning.

This most certainly does not mean establishing a forbidding atmosphere; in fact, everything should be done to avoid that. It does mean quiet planning that will make the session relaxed, a success. If you are to be the brainstorm leader, do your job well, but be unobtrusive. Don't tell everyone how much you've done, how hard you've worked. Brainstorming is a team effort. Don't try to take the credit. You'll get enough if the group comes up with good ideas, but like a good team captain, stay in the background yourself.

First step in setting up a successful brainstorm session is choosing the problem to be attacked. Its importance cannot be overestimated. I like to catalogue them as either steam-shovel or spade questions.

A steam-shovel question is a broad, general one. One I use in my lectures is, "How can we sell more gasoline in our service stations?" The biggest fault with that kind of question is that the answers are invariably steam-shovel answers, just as vague as the question. For example, the usual answers include: improve dealer training, have a better TV show, have faster service.

Another great fault of the steam-shovel question is that those who are attacking the problem aren't really shooting at the same target at all. They are not thinking about the same problem. One man is thinking about the city service station and another about the station in a resort area; one man is talking about evening sales, and another about truck sales. Their fire is scattered.

One way of fighting this problem is practiced by Harold Schmidhauser, Director of Executive Action courses at the American Management Association. He puts the question to be attacked on the blackboard, and then has everyone translate it into his own terms so that a workable definition is produced on the spot and the fire of the group concentrated on that definition.

Steam-shovel questions do have a place in brainstorming, however. Often they can dig out the problems you should attack. For example, you might brainstorm the steam-shovel question, "What obstacles stand in the way of increased gasoline sales in our service stations?" Then out of the hundred or so answers—poor salesmen on the pumps, dirty rest rooms, poor national advertising—you can apply judgment and pick out the problems which it is strategic to attack at the moment. Then brainstorm those.

In the same way a steam-shovel question can discover the boundaries of the problem. I once asked a steam-shovel question in a Pentagon session. It was, "How can you get more creative thinking in the Army?" The answers included: "Put out a staff directive," "Have the Signal Corps make a movie," "Get Congress behind it," and "Have a traveling demonstration team." From those steam-shovel questions you can get a clue to the real problem. One clue was to get creative thinking in the Pentagon. That was brainstormed, and of seventy-five ideas one was to have a lobby exhibit on creative thinking in the Pentagon. Then we brainstormed, "What would you put in a lobby exhibit in the Pentagon to stimulate creative thinking?" Then we were down to a spade question, and we got solid results.

A spade question is one that really digs into the problem. Brainstorming works best when it is directly oriented to action. It doesn't work at all well in answering such a judicial question as, "Should we set up a branch office in San Antonio?" It does work well when it is focused on, "What should our San Antonio office do to increase resubscriptions?"

Usually the first definition of a problem is a poor one. You have to work on it to hone it down to a good cutting edge. Recently I had a session in which the problem was first expressed as, "How can the accounting department improve its services to customers?" I asked what customers, and it was amended to read, "Wholesale and retail credit customers." Since that would split the fire of the group, I found out that retail customers were most important. So the question was reworded as, "How can the accounting department improve service to retail credit customers?" We got results.

The question should be worded in the shortest possible fashion, but at the same time it should be limited so the work of the brainstormers can be co-ordinated. For example, take the problem, "How can we build traffic in our service stations?"

That question has one good element. Professor C. C. Crawford of the University of Southern California has shown that a question starting with a "how" will get far greater results. But it still is pretty vague. We can limit by asking:

For whom? WOMEN DRIVERS? NEW DRIVERS? TRICK DRIVERS?

When? EVENINGS? HOLIDAYS? WINTER? SPRING?

Where? HIGHWAYS? IN SUBURBAN NEIGHBOR-HOODS? CITIES? FARMING COUNTRY?

By whom? SMALL STATIONS? GARAGES? LARGE STATIONS?

In this way get down to earth. You have a problem that people can really attack. They can see it, understand it, and therefore they can come up with practical solutions which can be put to work. And, strange to say, the wildest flights of fancy come from the most detailed, earthbound questions. The subconscious is like that.

Just about the most important factor in brainstorming is, of course, brains. Picking the right people is a crucial bit of planning that should be done with care.

Generally, all of those involved should have some familiarity with the problem, although not all of them should be experts. Sometimes the man directly responsible for its solution sits in, but some companies find that this inhibits other panel members who think they may seem to be criticizing Joe for not having their ideas. This is a real hazard, for often the best ideas are the obvious ones the person closest to the problem has not seen. And even if Joe doesn't yelp when someone mentions ideas he doesn't like, there are grunts, table tappings and glares that get the idea across.

To combat this, the man most responsible for the problem may be brought in to give a five-minute—no more—briefing or indoctrination on the problem. Then he leaves and the brainstorm begins.

What is desired is a potent mixture of specialties, attitudes, and backgrounds which will ignite when in contact with one another. Salesmen, shippers, distributors can help on a technical problem. Scientists, engineers, statisticians can help solve a sales problem. Unfortunately, some of my best friends are in the financial and accounting departments, but they rarely turn out to be good brainstormers, except when among their peers, and their professional scowls at the mention of an idea that might cost money can have a very red-light effect on other brainstormers. When these money men see the savings which can be made through brainstorming they very often come around and develop into fine brainstormers. Sometimes association with other workers on a brainstorm panel eliminates the scrooge stereotype of accountant, and thus the brainstorm can do a double service.

In general, an action group will do better than a broad policy committee in brainstorming, but this again tends more to be due to the questions asked than the basic make-up of the individuals. Actually, important policy questions, if they are really important, can be broken down into specifics. When a problem is vaguely defined, it's a pretty good rule that the real problem hasn't been found. Usually it is true, however, that the Board of Directors is a judicial group, passing on ideas, rather than thinking up ideas. It profits very greatly from brainstorms at a lower level, but does not itself brainstorm or originate ideas very often. Perhaps it should, and this may be a new horizon for brainstorms to cross. Some board of directors' meetings now end with a ten- or fifteen-minute brainstorm session after all the practical decisions have been made.

Some concerns have at least two to four women in every brainstorm, not only for the benefit of female brains—a very powerful ingredient indeed—but also for their stimulating effect on male panel members, who are needled on to better ideas by the Battle of the Sexes. Other companies like to invite outsiders who know nothing of company policy, economics, or history—and care less. These may be rather carefully chosen consultants, suppliers, customers, professors in the general field where the problem lies, or they may just be men off the street, friends who would be likely to provide a new look at an old problem. BBDO will invite traveling BBDO salesmen to brainstorm on a Sheraton Hotel problem, and some agency housewives when they are thinking up Campbell Soup ideas.

It's often a good idea to have groups of office boys, secretaries, file clerks, workers of all levels brainstorm a company problem. There are a number of good reasons for this. One is that they often have very good ideas. They see your problems differently because of their perspective. Another reason is that this can increase communication between all levels of management. Still another is that they can take part in management and enjoy a sense of participation.

To have absolute freedom during any brainstorm, however, it's best to pick individuals who are on the same approximate management level, so that there are no superiors and inferiors. Brass-polishing is not a function of a brainstorm.

No member of a panel should be able to place his job even slightly in danger by an unpopular idea or advance his stock by a bit of "Say, that's a fine idea"-ing after a superior has spoken.

It is also a good rule not to have the same group meet together all the time. There are several strong reasons for this. Groups who meet regularly usually evolve a pecking order. Joe can jump on Pete's ideas, but Pete can't strike back. Pete, however, can take a swing at Bob, and Bob can't swing at either Joe or Pete, and so on. Another reason is that there are hidden alliances; people who know where the bodies are buried and will use any momentary unwariness on the part of the opposition to advance their cause in the political hurly-burly of the office. Also, a group who has worked together on the same problems is too well aware of what has been tried and even what has been considered. It is generally unable to see that an old idea may be a new solution, especially if conditions have changed. Finally, the group tends to have an automatic reaction to ideas which slam the door in the face of opportunity.

There are strong exceptions to this; in fact, a company may almost by accident develop teams that seem to spark ideas again and again. BBDO has a basic core of idea men who seem to spark panels, and they sit in on many sessions with changing groups of brainstormers. Too often, however, such groups fall into a pattern in the same way that regular conferences often freeze into a sort of stereotyped mating dance with each person taking a predictable approach to the problem, and with the results being just as predictable. To combat this, when it is necessary to have the same group, some companies make the members of the panel sit in different chairs, and they have found that a varying geographical combination of people on one's right and left and across the table can make a difference in the level of creativity.

One important bit of planning for the brainstorm session is the invitation. Usually it's a good idea to phone first a week ahead and make sure the people you want are clear for the time you have planned. Since each panel is a small, specially chosen group, it can be disastrous if several members are out of town.

Beside the phone call there should be a written invitation which clearly shows the time, the place, and perhaps, if it is a new thing in the company, a casual line to show that it is important. "As you know, B.W. is behind this and anxious to see what we can do." Of course before you write that, in fact, before you start brainstorming, you should make darn sure B.W. *is* behind you. We'll take up that problem in another chapter.

In a regular conference the subject to be discussed is often kept secret. The participants are given a mysterious summons, one that is ominous and forbidding. It provides plenty of room for rumor, but little for constructive thought. "What's old fuddy-duddy up to today?" "Is Bill going to get fired?" "Is the market campaign going to be a flop?" This sort of conjecture is destructive and purposeless. There are other reasons that the secret type of summons is a waste of time and energy. It gives many people an excuse to put off work, saying, "Got to get to fuddy-duddy's conference." And above all, the summoned arrive devoid of ideas, but full of fear and fore-boding.

Once in the session, a problem is suddenly sprung on the assembled group. There is no chance to have your subconscious work over the problem, no opportunity to think up new ideas. Such conferences are generally a complete waste of time, and one of the reasons is a natural resentment of the way in which the conferees are being treated. The invitation to a brainstorming session must have the problem under attack clearly defined if the session is to be worth while. Everyone who attends the meeting should have been thinking about the problem and mulling it over. When they come into the brainstorm room they should be raring to attack it.

Another important point too many companies miss is that the invitation to a brainstorm session must be just that. It should be easy to turn down. That seems contradictory, but it isn't. It should not be a summons. People dragooned to a brainstorm session will hardly ever come up with good ideas. If the individuals invited would rather do other work, let them. Brainstorming will sell itself on results; it cannot be forced down people's throats. It is also wise to encourage the spirit expressed in, "I'd like to send my assistant over, he knows more about that problem than I do." The brainstorm session isn't being held to build up anyone's ego; it shouldn't be a sign of status. It is a sleeves-rolled-up work session designed to attack a problem in a hurry.

Here's a typical invitation to a brainstorm used by BBDO:

Date

(Have it reach participants two days before meeting)

To: Name of Participant

You are invited to a brainstorm on (date) at (place) at ——P.M.

The problem is as follows:

How Can We Increase the "Sale" of Home Extension Telephones? Extension telephones are available for any room in the house and cost either 70 or 80 cents a month plus an installation charge of about $2.50. Only about 16 per cent of the home telephones now have an extension, and the company is interested in selling the first one to most of the customers and additional ones to the old extension users.

Here are three examples of the kind of ideas we seek:

1   *Give an extension to mother as a Christmas gift. (You pay for the installation and the first year's cost.)*

2   *Make an arrangement with carpenters or contractors who do game room or workshop construction in basements. Let them give you names of people who are installing those facilities so you can call and try to sell an extension telephone for that room.*

3   *Prepare a sales piece to send to people when they inform you that they are moving. Sell the idea of having an extension installed at the same time that the new telephone is put in. This will save an installation charge for the extension.*

JOHN JONES
Chairman
Office Extension: 873

When brainstorming is new in the company, or when an individual is going to attend his first session, it may be well to introduce him to what brainstorming is by sending him some information about it with the invitation.

Many companies have booklets which define brainstorming, while others use extensive memos which are sent out to educate first-time brainstormers. The secret of such literature is that it should be specific. It must show clearly and with practical examples just how our thought processes work, why we can brainstorm, and how a brainstorm session works. To sell the idea of brainstorming to the reluctant employee, the literature must be spiced with practical, hard-cash results which highly respected concerns have received from brainstorming. After reading this, the new brainstormer should come to the meeting full of curiosity and enthusiasm, and in fact be grateful he has an opportunity to participate in this new adventure.

The invitation should clearly state the question to be brainstormed. This gives the subconscious a head start. Once the problem is firmly planted in the subconscious, it may chip away at the project as the individual walks through the plant, sees competitors' problems, flies to San Francisco to a sales convention, mows the lawn Saturday afternoon. When the brainstorm session is held he may be astonished to find what he has thought up.

Willard A. Pleuthner, BBDO's vice president in charge of brainstorming and communications, recommends that problems be stated as "think up new and different ways to . . ." He feels that this approach stimulates people to look for the unusual, the new ideas that will be outstanding because no one else is doing them that way.

In every case, when a proper question, a spade question, has been decided upon, and the members of the group have been told they will have to come up with new ideas, the subconscious seems to come through. It may, for example, rummage around in the brain attic called memory and come up with some of those good ideas that the participants had had but had never mentioned in old-style negative conferences for fear of being laughed at.

One company even suggests brainstormers come in with five ideas on the subject already written down to give the session a head start. Someone starts with an idea, others start hitch-hiking, and the session is off to a rousing beginning. Be sure not to let someone read all his ideas at once. That is deadly.

Whatever device is used, the invitation to the brainstorm should be on just one side of one sheet of paper, so the busy man who gets it will have time to read it right away, know the problem, the place, and the time. It's also a good idea to call his secretary to make sure it's marked on his calendar.

There is some debate about when brainstorming sessions should be held. The best answer is whenever they work. That isn't silly. That will change from group to group, business to business. Early in the day seems better than late, especially if you've got a pressure business where people get worn out, or if your members are commuters worried about catching the five-fifteen.

On the other hand, some young companies have their best brainstorms in evening sessions. Breakfast brainstorms have been successful, and even Sunday afternoon brainstorms around the nineteenth hole. Some general rules seem in order. Alcohol does usually release inhibitions, but the results are usually a waste of time. I don't know of a successful two-martini brainstorm. The ideas may seem brilliant to the participants, but they rarely work out. A big meal makes everyone sleepy and sluggish, not at all in the mood for quick mental gymnastics.

BBDO used to have breakfast or dinner brainstorm sessions; now they gather for a light soup break—Campbell's, of course—in the middle of the morning or a light lunch, with soup, in a room especially designed for the work, which has yellow walls, light wood table, and is packed with the solid results of previous brainstorm sessions.

The place can be important. Awhile back I was invited to lead a brainstorm session at one of New York's most venerable institutions. Seated around the massive mahogany table in the thick-carpeted board room, in great leather chairs, the members of the panel were constantly under the disapproving stares of the elders memorialized in oil portraits. No one could have offbeat, odd-ball ideas in that room. It would be sacreligious, and nobody did.

Atmosphere is important. Brainstorms can be held anywhere, but they should be held where the members of the group feel at ease. The members of the board in that same New York institution might have had a fine brainstorm in the board room in spite of the oiled elders, but not the lower level group gathered for that session. To them the room held the same awe as a throne room to the serfs in a medieval kingdom. By the same token, a New York Esso garage has remarkably successful brainstorms right in the middle of a busy shop. When they run into a problem, the foreman invites some of the boys over for a short coffee break, and they gather around the problem in hand. That certainly would be an atmosphere which would make the board members feel uncomfortable, but for the brainstorm it is just right.

The main thing is to find a room where the members of a particular brainstorming session will feel at ease. The room should not have the personality of the boss who can direct the future of the members. Everyone must feel free and easy. If it is necessary to sit in the boss's office, or a board room, then the senior members of the group must move away from their accustomed chairs, sit down the table instead of at the head of it. Sometimes it is best to move out of the company entirely to a room at a restaurant, hotel, or club, so there will be absolutely no tangible reminder of inhibiting company policies.

No matter where the brainstormers gather, it is always a good idea to have physical examples of the problem at hand, if possible. If packaging is the problem under question, then have the product and some packaging material where it can be seen, touched, bent, torn.

There are as many ways as the imagination can devise to increase the creative atmosphere of a brainstorming session. One is to have charts on the wall showing the number of positive, profitable results from other brainstorms. Another is to have a green traffic light, either in actual model form or on a poster to remind the individuals that this is a green-light session, and everything goes.

Some companies even have brainstorming rooms with

bright yellow paint on the walls, since scientists have ascertained that yellow is conducive to creativeness.

A bit of music to introduce a change of pace from the regular business atmosphere can be useful. Modern art can make people see in different terms. I have often thought short movies which might show our world from the high perspective of a helicopter or the low perspective of a child might be very useful. For example, a company wanting to discover ways to sell children's food better in a supermarket, might show a picture of a supermarket as seen from the height of a four-year-old, the age that tugs at mother's skirts and pleads, "Let's buy that, Mommy, let's hey, Mommy, please, hey, can I, hey, will you?"

Whatever you do, find a place which will make the brainstormers feel free to attack the problem, no holds barred.

KEEP 'EM ROLLING

*how you can learn
to be a good
brainstorm
chairman*

*the list of outlawed
killer phrases*

*one of
apologetic phrases*

*what the
secretary does*

*how to catch
ideas*

*tricks to keep
ideas coming*

*what you
can do
about
that terrible
long silence*

You can't brainstorm if you don't know what brainstorming is.

Obvious? Silly? Unnecessary? Of course. But time after time people come to me after a lecture and say, "We tried brainstorming, and it just won't work in our situation."

When I talk to them I find out that they don't know what brainstorming is. Some of them call it brainwashing. One even said they could not barnstorm at his company. None of them caught the concept of uninhibited idea making.

This is the responsibility of the chairman. If he has a group which has never brainstormed, then he has to explain what brainstorming is.

His talk should be short. It must be dramatic, and it must hammer home the basic principles of creative thinking which we cover in this book: that we have a judicial mind which is logical, and a creative mind which is illogical; that we need both, but that too often our judicial mind completely dominates our creative mind; because of that fact many successful concerns are using a technique called brainstorming, in which judgment is ruled out; that everyone contributes any idea which occurs to him, and that later, after the session is over, the judicial mind goes to work on the list.

There are many ways for the chairman to get this across. He can use this book and develop a short presentation. I have a "Do-it-yourself Brainstorm Kit" designed to do the job, which consists of twelve four-color, flip-flop charts, a word-by-word script, a printed introduction to brainstorming, a bell, materials to use to orient first-time brainstormers. This kit was developed after tests before ninety-five groups from coast to coast, and it is used in many executive development programs, sales training courses, management training schools. It costs twenty-five dollars plus shipping charges and can be ordered from Creative Thinking Courses, Inc., 11 West 42nd Street, New York 36, N.Y.

Quite often I have the members, in turn, read out loud the rules for brainstorming as stated on page 70. Thus, in their own words by repetition, the fact is impressed on the members that this is a green-light session. I usually display a green traffic light or a green circle of cardboard to dramatize the idea.

The most dramatic way I know to show how most conferences are negative and firmly opposed to new ideas is to have each member of the group write on three-by-five cards three killer phrases, such as: "It's against policy," "It won't work," "We've never done it before," "The boss's wife likes blue." Then I have the cards shuffled and passed around in the group. They are read aloud by panel members.

On the following pages there is a list of the most prevalent killer phrases. You know them well; everyone does who has ever attended a meeting, but read the list over carefully. You will hear echoes from wasted conferences, and you will know what to avoid in the future. In a brainstorm session killer phrases are strictly ruled out. In fact, I place a bell in the center of the table, and whenever a killer phrase pops up the bell is rung by the person nearest it.

Here they are:

We've never done it that way before . . .

It won't work . . .

We haven't the time . . .

We haven't the manpower . . .

It's not in the budget . . .

We've tried that before . . .

We're not ready for it yet . . .

All right in theory but can you put it into practice?

Too academic . . .

What will the customers think?

Somebody would have suggested it before if it were any good . . .

Too modern . . .

Too old-fashioned . . .

Let's discuss it at some other time . . .

You don't understand our problem . . .

We're too small for that . . .

We're too big for that . . .

We have too many projects now . . .

Let's make a market research test first . . .

It has been the same for twenty years so it must be good . . .

What bubblehead thought that up?

I just know it won't work . . .

Let's form a committee . . .

Let's think it over for a while and watch developments . . .

That's not our problem . . .

Production won't accept it . . .

They'll think we're long-haired . . .

Engineering can't do it . . .

Won't work in my territory . . .

Customers won't stand for it . . .

You'll never sell that to management . . .

CHAPTER FIVE

Don't move too fast . . .
Why something new now? Our sales are still going up . . .
Let's wait and see . . .
The union will scream . . .
Here we go again . . .
Let's put it in writing . . .
I don't see the connection . . .
Won't work in our industry . . .
We can't do it under the regulations . . .
Nuts . . .
Political dynamite . . .
Sounds good but don't think it will work . . .
It's not in the plan . . .
No regulations covering it . . .
We've never used that approach before . . .
It's not in the manual . . .
It'll mean more work . . .
It's not our responsibility . . .
Yes, but . . .
It will increase overhead . . .
It's too early . . .
It's too late . . .
It will offend . . .
It won't pan out . . .
Our people won't accept it . . .
You don't understand the problem . . .
No adolescent is going to tell me how to run my business . . .

Beside the killer phrase, you have to ring the bell on the killer glance and the man who jumps at repetition. Repeating an idea may spark a new chain reaction.

A twin brother to the killer phrase someone else uses to swat

your idea is the apologetic phrase you often use to give a
deadly introduction to your own idea. In a brainstorm session
it's outlawed too, but don't ring the bell. Notice how these
killers disappear as you cultivate a creative atmosphere receptive to new ideas. Edward J. Walsh of General Foods calls
these "Self-Killer Phrases."

Can you hear yourself in this list? If you can, discipline
yourself to present ideas not with apology but with confidence.

This may not be applicable, but . . .
While we have only made a few preliminary tests . . .
This may not work, but . . .
This approach is screwy, but . . .
It isn't clear that we need this, but . . .
I don't know if the money can be appropriated, but . . .
It might be a dead end, but . . .
Would it hurt if we did . . .
Do you suppose it would be possible to . . .
It may sound hair-brained, but . . .
It may take a long time, but . . .
I don't know just what you want, but . . .
You probably have ideas about this too, but . . .
You aren't going to like this, but . . .
This is contrary to policy, but . . .
This may not be the right time, but . . .
This idea seems useless, but . . .
You can probably do this better, but . . .
If I was younger and had my health . . .
I suppose our competitors have already tried this, but . . .
I'm not too familiar with this, but . . .
This may be too expensive, but . . .

I don't know what is in the literature on this, but . . .
This is not exactly on this subject, but . . .
I haven't thought this one through, but . . .
You'll probably laugh, but . . .
My opinions are not worth much, but . . .
I'm no genius, but . . .
Perhaps we can't sell this to the old man, but . . .
I don't get enthused over this idea myself, but . . .
It may not be important, but . . .
This will need further study, but . . .
If you'll take the suggestion of a novice . . .
I'm not aware of all the complexities of the issue, but . . .
Joe doesn't agree with me, but . . .
I realize this doesn't solve the problem, but . . .
If I'm out of line, correct me, but . . .
Now here's a sketchy idea of what I have in mind, for you
to kick holes in . . .

The brainstorm session is not the time for apologies or modesty; it is not the time for cold water or wet blankets. The chairman must stop the use of all killer phrases. By ringing the bell and having others ring the bell as soon as one is heard, he can do it with humor but with telling effect. Once the danger of the killer phrase is pointed out, most of us try to avoid the habit, but they are so much a part of our conference personality we need a reminder to retrain ourselves into thinking creatively, positively instead of negatively.

One other thing that must be made clear by the chairman is that hitch-hiking on someone else's idea is not only permissible, it is very much cricket. One company hands out clickers with which a person can get attention to hitch-hike, others have people rap on the table. This hitch-hike system encourages the crackling chain reaction of ideas. For example, here are a few from a brainstorm session on vitalizing tearoom modeling at Halle Brothers department store in Cleveland, Ohio, one of the most creative retailers and successful users of brainstorming in the country.

Model more bathing suits.
More men's clothing should be modeled.
More children's wear should be modeled.

Models should travel the entire tearoom.

Increase the size of the platform—a bed on it to demonstrate contour sheets—or display other appliances on this enlarged platform.

Fix platform as a room—a more interesting background for both models and appliances.

Place organ on platform—get customers to come up on platform to play the organ—to start the ball rolling, plant a few people in the audience.

Model clothes for mother-to-be.

Have child and doll dresses alike model in tearoom.

To promote yard goods—have model drape material around body.

Have model drape several swatches over arm.

Around-the-clock day—have models wear in sequence—bathrobe and curlers, shower and bath apparel, house dresses, shopping and market clothes, polo coat, working in the garden, lunch dress, afternoon dress, evening apparel, etc.

A brainstorm session isn't a place to be polite. No one should drown out the other members, but there should be no hesitation in speaking out, right on the end of another idea. One idea will tumble right on top of another.

This is the pattern, and therefore there is an easy way to handle the floor-holder. In a regular conference he is never headed off. The Niagara of words is not halted by polite throat clearings, "Well, Joe, that's right, but . . ." interruptions, or feet shufflings. In the brainstorm session the chairman can cheerfully interrupt him by saying, "Fine, now another one," "Please get it in one or two sentences," or even by slamming the bell. If he insists on holding the floor, don't invite him next time. There's a deadline, and there are ideas to be born.

Brainstorms are not long-drawn-out conferences. They are quick commando attacks which can be fitted into the dozen busy schedules of the participants. Since judgment will come later, there is no need for the long-drawn-out discussions, debates, feuds, diplomatic language, and the ploymanship of the regular conference. Ideas are not to be sold, defended, or attacked. In a brainstorm ideas are merely tossed on the table to be sorted out and discussed later.

The most productive brainstorm session in history would be wasted if there was not an efficient way to capture every idea. The best ideas, in fact, quite often would be forgotten. Because of the very nature of brainstorming, the members are not trying to catch and evaluate ideas, but rush on to the next one.

The best system, I believe, is to have a stenographer who takes down every idea as it comes along. She should sit near the chairman as he presides, since she is catching every idea. Catching each word is not important; catching the idea is. The most important thing is that any secretary does not, even unconsciously, clean up the ideas by not taking down ideas which he or she thinks are obviously ridiculous, just silly jokes. And she must record them all, even repeaters. Judgment of any kind, even by the secretary, must be ruled out. Her job is to record.

A member of the group can be the secretary, but that pretty much rules out that person as an idea maker, for when the ideas flow thick and fast it will be a job to keep up with them. In fact, some companies use two recorders to keep up with the flood. If you use two, have them sit on opposite sides of the table and record ideas from the people whose faces they can see on the opposite side of the table. This will eliminate confusion and increase accuracy. Tape-recorders can be used, of course, but inexperienced operators can make errors in operation, and few office-type machines have microphones which will pick up every word as ideas tumble on top of each other. Some companies use a blackboard to capture ideas. It does give everybody a chance to see the whole list and elicits new combinations of ideas, but it slows the process down dangerously, in my opinion.

It is a good rule *not* to note who has what idea. Brainstorm sessions are not the place for grandstanding; this kind of brainstorming calls for team play, where one idea ignites another—or modifies, changes, expands it. The brainstormers should seek group recognition, not individual reward. There is one exception, however. In some technical fields where patents are involved, the secretary may initial each idea and keep those initials with the ideas, so if a record is needed, it is there.

Johnson & Johnson have each idea suggested by a woman

marked, so that when the company has a product sold to women they give more weight to the woman's ideas. Again, remember that my suggestions are just that. Work out your own system, the one best suited to your particular problem.

Sometimes brainstorm sessions come to a complete stop. There are many ways to handle this. One is by establishing a deadline. Every brainstorm session should have a time limit, at first not more than twenty minutes from beginning to end. The deadline must be observed, unless ideas are flowing hot and heavy, of course. Sometimes it can be extended, for example, "We have eighty-seven ideas, let's see if we can break one hundred." Generally, however, the session should stop on schedule. Willard A. Pleuthner reports that BBDO found that with experienced brainstormers they can run a 30 to 45 minutes session at coffee break and a 45 to 60 minutes session at a soup-and-sandwich luncheon.

There is a most serious hazard in not having a deadline. If there is a lull, it's natural to assume that the period of productivity is over and to call it quits. I have found that periods of silence are followed by great bursts of ideas; a premature ending can sacrifice these ideas.

Some brainstorm leaders try to produce a contagious enthusiasm, acting as a cheerleader. Some root during silences, "Come on, team, let's go." They may even wave their arms, come up with their own ideas, encourage tentative ones, carrying the group with them. Others are auctioneers, chanting, "We've sixty, let's try for seventy, who'll make it eighty?" It actually works in some cases. But I think it is unnecessary.

I've found that silences may naturally occur, even in the most productive sessions. After a spate of ideas the silences may be sudden and disconcerting, but actually, although they may seem to last long, they don't. Don't be afraid of dead air. Wait patiently, and if the group appears restive, you may say, "We're doing fine. We've got plenty of time." But if the group doesn't worry about the silence, the leader shouldn't. The subconscious is an undisciplined animal, and soon it will dart off and the session will be rolling again.

Sometimes when a session does seem to come to a real dead end, however, the chairman can throw in an idea he has saved to trigger the group. If I don't do that I have the secretary slowly read every second or third item on the list to start the session going again on new categories. Everyone is invited to interrupt with ideas, and usually the session goes charging off again before the secretary is finished.

To prime a session or get it warmed up, some outfits have each member write ideas on separate slips of paper, then they are in the mood—and they have ammunition to use if the session bogs down.

One of the best ways to perk up a really stalled session is to go over the rules for having new ideas, or at least new variations on ideas. I will deal with that list in detail later. But here, briefly, is my technique.

First I ask everyone to add something to the problem, then to subtract from it, finally to multiply or divide. This encourages members to look at the problem in a new light. It is an artificial trick, of course, but it is surprising how often this technique can be used to spark a chain reaction of new ideas. For example, the session might be trying to solve the problem of how to sell a kneehole desk for the home. By adding to it you might come up with some ideas such as these:

You might throw in a chair on a sale, or a desk blotter, or an attractive student lamp, or give the desk to purchasers of a special typewriter. In other words, you might solve the problem by adding to it. Then you might solve the problem by subtracting. The desk may have been promoted as part of a set of furniture for a teen-ager's bedroom. You might subtract it from that set and promote it as a single unit to be used by a student at college, or for a housewife's home record center, or for Dad's den. Then you might try to multiply the problem, for example, how many desks can one home use? This can be used by Junior for his homework, another desk might be used in the corner of a kitchen by a housewife, or in Grandma's room, who keeps the family together through voluminous letter-writing, and so on, so that you could get ideas on how to sell a second or third desk to a family. Then again you might divide the problem. How many uses can a kneehole desk have? It can be used as a chest or checker table in the corner of a living room, as a hobby center in the family room, for sewing materials in Mother's alcove. As you divide the problem you will see many new possible solutions of the single problem of how to sell a particular kneehole desk.

If adding, subtracting, multiplying, or dividing the problem doesn't work, then you can try what I call the "else" type of question. You can ask yourself "who else," "where else," "why else," "when else," "what else" would solve it. For example, you might say "what else" would get the suburban housewife into the service station, and come up with other lures—recipes, dress patterns, or kitchen decals—which would be given away with a lubrication job and oil change.

Finally, if none of those things work, I try to think of

"alikes" and "unlikes" to start a chain reaction of thought. I might run through a list of things other businesses have done to attract women customers, or even things that have been done to attract men customers. What I am trying to do in every case is to stimulate my subconscious so that it will hit on new categories.

The introduction of those rules, even if an artificial technique, often jogs brainstormers into new mental associations and exercises.

I also tell them to reverse the problem by looking at it from the inside out, upside down, or backward. Any problem can be thought of in a hundred different concepts; seen from a hundred different points of view. For example, if you are trying to solve the problem of how to shoot down enemy planes and can't come up with any new ideas, you might attack the problem this way. How can our planes most easily be shot down? Through seeing your own vulnerability you might spot the enemy's. Or take another case closer to our daily life; if you are trying to solve the problem of keeping Junior from writing on walls, you might find the best solution by posing the problem, "Where can Junior have fun learning to write and draw?"

Some brainstorm leaders have the members of a blocked session get up and walk around the room, even have them take different seats. Some schedule a brief smoke break in which other subjects are discussed. Obviously the subconscious keeps on working and is ready to produce ideas at the end of the break.

Harold Schmidhauser of the American Management Association runs his sessions for only three minutes. At the end of that time he has a break. During that period no one talks about the problem or consciously thinks about it. Then they go into another three-minute session. Still another break follows that one, and then they return for an additional three-minute brainstorm.

There's no limit to the ways you might develop this idea. I do not think you should interrupt a session that is really rolling along, but if one is blocked or slowed down, then you might call a halt to read a paragraph or two of some material which might inspire ideas on the subject under attack. For example, brainstormers trying for ideas on how to improve motel business might have their subconscious inspired by a rather romantic piece on the open road, which would get them thinking like travelers and thus make them see what they would look for in a place to stop for the night.

Music, pictures, special magazine articles, slides, movies, or even a walk out to the shipping room or production line where the problem exists might do the trick. I've long thought a museum with models of good ideas from the past, or even a trophy room or shelf of ideas the company has brainstormed before might be a powerful stimulus to a stalled session. Willard Pleuthner gets ideas back on the track by asking participants to reread the problem which he has displayed on a large sign or blackboard.

Just the opposite of the stalled session is the one which charges off on a wild tangent. If you have a proper question this will not happen as much as you might think. If it does, however, I like to toss in an idea which will get the group back to the problem at hand. If I don't have such an idea, then I have the secretary read the list at a point before the group stampeded. This usually gets the ideas back down to earth.

You must be extremely careful about this, however. You may think the group is off on a tangent, when it actually is developing a new and brilliant line of attack on an old problem. Be of open mind about tangents and haul the group back on base only when it is necessary. Then do it with kid gloves so they will not be inhibited from having other tangential ideas.

The important thing in all this is never to panic when the group charges off wildly or stalls. Remember that brainstorming is a sure producer of usable ideas. In my travels around the country brainstorming I have found that a good group of twelve men can easily come up with 60 to 110 ideas in twenty-five minutes. In following up the sessions I discovered that a predictable return of eight to a dozen usable ideas will come out of every hundred. That's a solid 8–12 per cent return on your investment of time and effort, a good solid business profit in any man's league.

AFTER THE STORM IS OVER

*what you do
after the
brainstorm*

*how you
can collect
extra ideas*

*what to do
with your ideas*

*who applies
judgment*

the screened list

At last the deadline is met. The brainstorm session is over. Its members pile out of the room; the secretaries stretch their fingers before picking up the long list of ideas. But the brainstorm process is far from finished. Ideas, even the best ideas in the world, are useless unless they are put to work.

Turning ideas into action must be an integral part of the brainstorming session, or else it will be a complete waste of time. You can dream up the best toaster in the world, have the best automobile design in your head, discover the formula for a miracle drug, but if you don't get your product to the public you are a failure.

Ideas can't be stored up like bars of gold. They can't be hoarded. They are only valuable when they are turned into action, into products, services, beliefs. The brainstormer's job is not over when the brainstormers slap each other on the back and leave the room.

To make sure they have collected every possible idea, some companies have a panel member call the others twenty-four hours after a meeting, to ask for all ideas they have had on the way home, while sleeping or shaving. Rarely has their subconscious stopped working.

After all the ideas have been collected, a secretary types a triple-spaced list exactly as the ideas came in the session. Then the chairman reads that list, expanding the ideas which need it, and adding other ideas which occur to him. He then organizes the list into categories. For example, he might organize a list putting together all the ideas about retail sales, wholesale promotion, advertising, etc. The categories should correspond to the logical ones for your business and your problems.

That organized list is typed and duplicated. It is sent to every member of the brainstorm session. Some concerns write each person who gets a list to add any additional ideas, perhaps with just a note to the chairman—"Joe, saw the list, how about fish sticks? Pete."

This list is important. It makes everyone aware of what has been done in what may seem to critics a rather ephemeral operation. It gets ideas down on paper. This makes them a positive force within the organization. For example, for years a company has been trying to cut shipping costs. The brainstorm session produced 107 ideas. They are possible solutions to the problem: twelve people from seven departments had them. The president and the top people in the concern have seen them. They have to be acted upon, rejected perhaps, but only with a reason. And each member of the panel is likely to feel some proprietorship over their results. Therefore the reasons for rejection had better not just be killer phrases!

This does not mean that any of the ideas have to be utilized. It does mean that there is a pressure to try new ideas, or at least consider them, which counterbalances the natural inertia in any organization which resists change.

Often the list will produce an idea or ideas that can be brainstormed profitably themselves. This is especially true when the question in the first session is a steam-shovel one. Then the group can reconvene after having fifty-eight vague ideas on how to increase sales of dog food, and attack specific proposals for contacting veterinarians, setting up supermarket displays, reaching children through TV shows. Then the sessions will not come up with fifty-eight ideas. The total is more likely to be 158.

Now that the ideas have been produced, judgment must be applied to the ideas in a vigorous, cold-water session. This may be done by the entire group in a technique worked out by Professor Paul Pigors at M.I.T. He has found that a brainstorm panel can immediately sort their own ideas into three categories: (1) hot ideas that can be tried out almost immediately; (2) those which need long range or involved study, co-ordination, or vast appropriations; (3) those which are obviously unusable. General Electric's Royce plant in Toronto arranges their ideas into those which can be put to work: (1) in one week; (2) one month; (3) six months, and so on.

To have the whole group do the judging, of course, takes a great deal more time than the session itself, and it completely wastes the time of those nonexperts who just don't know enough about the subject to say if an idea is practical or not.

It is best to have a committee of about three panel members, usually the ones most concerned with the problem, meet and apply judgment. They should be the folks who know what has been tried, what is too expensive, what's against policy. To save time in this session each committee member should read over the list beforehand and come in with the top ten ideas. Usually the committee will find it quickly agrees on a majority.

This part of the brainstorm process should not be underestimated. This is the time when common sense, experience, and sound business judgment come into play. When you use brainstorming, you do not and should not throw away years of experience. The purpose of brainstorming is to provide you and your company with new ideas and with an atmosphere in which new ideas are encouraged. But they must be executed with every bit of your professional skill.

When you look at a brainstorm list of 150 ideas, you will see that many of them do not fit the problem. Now is the time for negative thinking. Your committee should have someone who is familiar with what the company and the industry have tried.

As you look at a list you will see, perhaps, that a dozen or so of the ideas have been tested in the research department and found not practical. Others may not fit your methods of distribution, your budget, your manufacturing capacity. There may be ideas that go against company policy or industry ethics. There may be a good idea that a competitor has tried and that just doesn't work out. You should and must be familiar with all these things.

The person who screens the list must be aware of what your company has done to try to solve the problem under attack, but he must not only know the history of the problem in your company, he must know it in the whole industry. No company should waste its time trying out all sorts of ideas that have been tried before. The person who is screening the list must seek out the new and practical ideas which can solve the problem.

This can be a tricky business. The value of the brainstorm session would be lost if blanket negative judgment were applied. The person who screens the list must be open-minded enough to be able to see if a possible solution has been given a fair trial previously. *He must be able to differentiate quickly between a screwball idea and the unorthodox one which is really creative.*

Often an idea from a brainstorm session may include in it a factor which makes a previously unsuccessful idea potentially successful. This is why the ideas must be taken down verbatim and not cleaned up by the secretary. For example, if the problem being brainstormed were one on how to stop damage of your product when it is being shipped, one of the session members might suggest crating it—an old idea, and one that has proved too expensive—but he also might mumble something about staples. That might be the key to the design of a crate which could be quickly and cheaply assembled with a staple gun. Or take another case: you might have the idea for a new product, a good idea, which has always been unprofitable in the past, but which might be very profitable if it is made of a newly developed plastic.

The man who does the screening, therefore, must combine a great deal of experience with a still vigorous and youthful approach to his work. He must, in other words, be a man of good judgment, able to distinguish the old from the new, the practical from the impractical, the impossible from the possible.

When the individual or the committee screens the list and comes up with the top ten ideas, then the committee decides the next steps to be taken. Should the solution be studied further, should it be bucked over to a specialist, to a consulting firm, or should the company reference library be consulted to see if some similar solutions have been tried? The committee should also decide if test models are to be made, or trials run.

This is also the time to decide to whom the ideas should be passed, to what level of management, or to what executive for decision and implementation. If proper aim is not taken, the whole virtue of the brainstorm session can be lost. The committee should also decide what form should be used to present the idea, and many times it will also brainstorm the best way in which to sell the idea.

Then the chairman reports to the brainstorm members. He should tell them, by memo, how many ideas are being acted upon. There is no reason to tell them which ideas or why ideas have been chosen or rejected. That only starts wasteful debate or discussion. He should make sure that they know something has been done with their ideas.

It is wise to pass only a screened list to the boss. If he sees ninety-eight ideas and is busy, he may read ten, twenty, or even thirty, say, "This is nuts," and hurl it into the waste-basket. The forty-third idea is one that might have increased his business by a million dollars or more.

Give him a screened list of only the very best ideas. If he wants the whole list, give it to him later. But first present him with the best ideas. Save his time, and sell him on brainstorming at the same time. The ideas you give him should be on one side of a paper and only one idea to a page, so he can act on it immediately, initialing it, and shooting it along the proper channels for action.

Remember that the brainstorm session is not a flighty affair. Sound, professional judgment must be applied to the ideas, and all the skill and experience you have at your command must be used to turn them into fact. If you do this, if you follow through all the way, you will find that brainstorming has a fabulous pay-off.

IDEAS? IN MY COMPANY?

*how to sell
brainstorming
to your boss*

*the best way to
sell a superior*

*how you can
sell new ideas
in your company*

*the strategy
and tactics
you can use
to turn your ideas
into action*

Before you sell your company, you've got to sell yourself. You've got to know all about brainstorming, you've got to know how it works, and you've got to know it *does* work.

You can't just stroll into H.L.'s office and say, "Hey, I heard about a way to get new ideas, called brainstorming."

You can predict his answer. At best it'll be a "What?" If you wander off in generalizations about brainstorming, if you don't have sharp, specific answers—and even sharper and more specific results, he won't pay any attention to you. The best way, of course, is never to go to H.L. at all, but to have him come to you and say, "I like those new ideas of yours. Where are you getting 'em?"

You can get old H.L. to come to you if you plan your strategy well. The first thing to do is to find out all about brainstorming. Read this book thoroughly. Read other articles on the subject. If neighboring concerns are using brainstorming, talk to them; perhaps you can even sit in on a session. Maybe the college nearby teaches creative thinking. See if they have an expert on brainstorming, ask him to let you sit in on a few classes.

Once you know what a brainstorm session is, try it on for size. Try it with your family and friends. Use it as a parlor game. Train yourself to suspend judgment in facing a problem, and be convinced by results you yourself get that brainstorming can and will pay off in cold, hard ideas.

Even after you have tried it out and know it will work, don't drag it into the company and toss it defiantly on old H.L.'s desk. Start modestly at your own level. You might have a brainstorm in the car pool on how to work out a better commuting schedule, or brainstorm at lunch on what to give Joe as a bowling prize. Get a few men together to brainstorm in small and informal ways. Once they learn what brainstorming is, try it out on specific company problems.

This does not mean top policy problems. It means how to make better use of the new milling machine, or how to sell your product to Acme Roller Bearings, or how to pack the product in cardboard instead of wood. Get some good ideas and act on them. H.L.'ll hear about you, have no fear of that. Brainstorming is a potent weapon. It will turn out so many ideas that they will draw attention to you and the men you are brainstorming with. Then you'll have H.L. coming to you —not about brainstorming, but about ideas. Alex F. Osborn suggests that you show examples of how other companies in your field are successfully using brainstorming.

What, you laugh, H.L. isn't interested in new ideas! Well, maybe not. But he is interested in three thousand dollars saved, in a new and profitable way of producing gludgets, of landing a new account, of solving shipping, sales, and production problems. He won't be seeing new ideas. He'll be seeing hard-headed profitable solutions to tough problems. He'll be seeing brainstorming at work, and he'll be interested, never you fear.

If you have a boss who is still sternly opposed to new ideas and to new ways of getting them, then the best way to sell brainstorming is to brainstorm that very problem. Establish a good spade question: "How can I sell brainstorming to

H.L.?" The more specific the better. Set your target up, and you'll know certain factors—that H.L. likes written memos, or he listens to proposals; that he likes to solve packing problems himself, or everything has to be expressed in sales to mean anything to him. Once you have established who you have to sell, then your brainstorm will give you plenty of ideas how.

Glenn Cowan, director of work simplification at B. F. Goodrich, recommends that you pick the "burr under the saddle," the problem which is most irritating to your boss. Solve that and you'll get his attention.

Most people spend 95 per cent of their time thinking up ideas, less than five per cent thinking what to do with them. I think you ought to spend at least a third of your time producing ideas on how to put your ideas to work. There are all sorts of ways to do this. For example, you might take the list of killer phrases in Chapter 5 and write them down, one each on three-by-five cards. The evening before you take your new idea in to the boss, have your wife read the killer phrases to you—"It costs too much," "It isn't practical," "It's been done before," and so on—then limber up your arguments by answering each killer phrase.

But first, let's run over some of the tactics you might use to sell the idea of brainstorming to your boss. You could find out, for example, which competitors are using the technique, and when he roars, "Where in blank did the Acme Pistol Release Company come up with that idea?" you could answer, "They probably brainstormed it," and explain how they have been using it. Or you might try it in your own department in a modest way, and once you have established a pattern of solid results, show them to him. You could keep mentioning brainstorming at staff meetings, but only if you have well-documented results, and by the same token you can invite him to brainstorm demonstrations given by business groups, but again, only if you know they will be good ones. You can also shoot magazine articles about brainstorming across his desk.

Another way to sell the idea to him is to list specific company problems that could be solved by brainstorming, and perhaps attach to it a list of new ideas other companies have used to solve their problems.

One of the most effective ways to sell brainstorming is to demonstrate it on his favorite or most irritating problem. If he suddenly finds himself with a list of 165 solutions to his pet peeve, he'll become extremely interested in brainstorming. A twist on this, which has worked out, is to challenge him to submit a problem for a private demonstration. This is especially good on the I'm-from-Missouri type who has to be shown.

Of course, you should always show how brainstorming can make money for the company, and at the same time tell him that it will cost the company no money to try brainstorming. One company I know underlined this by showing how much it cost them not to have the ideas they might have received from brainstorming.

You know your boss best. You may have to appeal to his secretary, his wife, the men closest to him. You may have to make him think it was his idea; you may have to camouflage it under a different name. But if you sit down and think carefully, you will see which approach is best. Personally, I like the one which stood out in my mind from a list of 308 ideas we got in a six-minute mass brainstorm I ran at the American Management Association on "How to Sell Brainstorming to Executives." Here it is in its entirety: "Do it! Don't ask!"

Remember, if you want to sell brainstorming, or any other idea, that solid results will make the difference. Start with a couple of people attacking clear-cut and basic company problems. Then add a third person, then a fourth, building up a team who enjoys brainstorming and believes in it. Attack specific problems and you'll come up with specific solutions— and the successful problem solver is too valuable a man to be ignored in any organization.

The same general rules hold true for selling any idea to your boss. But here are the results of a large number of brainstorms I have held around the country with top executives. I shall summarize what we have discovered, and from them you can develop an idea bank from which you can draw when you have difficulty putting a new idea across.

First, appeal to his motives. One way to do this is to show how it will help him save his time, cut down his headaches, get the jump on his personal competition. You might also subtly indicate that he will get the credit for it, that it is the kind of idea his boss usually likes, and you might even butter him up a bit by telling him he will get a reputation for being a forward thinker, and that obviously his predecessor never had the foresight to do it.

You can also appeal to his motives by showing how it will help his department, improve quality, increase production, cut costs, get more customers, and so on and on, depending on what he is trying to do in his job.

You should also provide assurances; you can show him there is already a demand for it and acceptance of this technique by his superiors. You might prove to him that it won't mean any more work for him, perhaps by offering to see it through yourself. You also can assure him that it is worth while by showing the results of a pilot run or by revealing the results other companies have had.

You must properly present the idea. Work up a sales presentation. Wait till you have the facts to do a solid job of selling, then present it in the way he will be most receptive—on the nineteenth hole, at lunch, during a flying trip to Wichita, at the office. You must be sure that you approach him in the right direction—through his fair-haired boy, his secretary, wife, or friend.

Again, let him think it's his idea. Don't overtalk or oversell. Once he begins to see the advantages of it, let him pick up the ball and run with it.

Remember all the way that your company may not want ideas, it may be scared of creative thinking, of change or variety. But it does want its problems solved, its profits increased, its competitive position improved. When you can produce solid results from brainstorming, brainstorming will sell itself.

THE PREACHING PRACTICED

*actual case histories
of brainstorm
sessions*

the invitation

the line-up

*the brainstorm
itself*

the list of ideas

cold cash results

Seeing is believing. Now that I've talked about brainstorming, I'm going to take you to see an actual brainstorm session, but first, I'm going to run through a model brainstorm session. We will see how one concern used brainstorming, and follow some of the elements which make a successful brainstorming session.

Here's the situation: The *Metropolitan News* is a large city newspaper, which comes out in the morning and has most of its circulation in the suburban area. With the competition from other media, such as radio, TV, magazines, and other papers, the *News* has to scramble to maintain its good business position. It is carrying on a vigorous campaign to build circulation, and one of the techniques it has used to get new ideas in all areas of its operation is brainstorming. The publisher's assistant, Charlie Douglas, has been assigned a number of areas as his responsibility. One is circulation.

He decides to hold a brainstorm on circulation problems. He knows that a brainstorm is most effective if it attacks a specific problem, and therefore he sits at his desk one morning and on a long yellow pad lists their circulation problems. One is how to get more circulation in the city, as the city grows toward the suburbs. He narrows the subject down until he comes up with this target, "How to increase our weekday morning circulation in the city."

One man, Fritz Dalton, an assistant circulation manager, has been charged with this problem, so Douglas decides not to have him attend the session, since he might inhibit the other people from coming up with ideas which might seem to infer criticism of Fritz. Instead he has the circulation expert come in and make a five-minute talk on the problem at the beginning of the session. Douglas has his secretary check with Fritz and clear the date. It's okay.

Then Douglas picks his panel. When he gets through with the first list he sends it to his secretary. She calls the names on the list, or their secretaries, and makes sure they are free at the time of the meeting. When they are not, Douglas picks an appropriate substitute. The final panel includes himself, a production man who lives in the city area where they want to sell more papers, two advertising solicitors who have come up with good ideas before, the city editor, whose job it is to know the city inside out, two young circulation men who are out on the streets talking to subscribers all the time, an old-time circulation man who deals with the downtown newspaper dealers, a sports writer who has a well-earned reputation for taking an offbeat approach to problems, and a police reporter who works the early morning shift. He also invites the production boss, who knows all the technical details about getting the paper on the streets, and the promotion man who will have to sell any campaigns or changes which come about as a result of the brainstorm session. Looking over the list next morning, he realizes that he has ignored the woman reader. He invites the woman's editor, a married woman who lives with her husband and two children in a fashionable apartment, and his secretary, who is single and lives in a women's hotel.

Next he writes out an invitation which he has mimeographed on plum-colored paper so that everyone who is attending will be sure to see it. In it he merely says, "As you know, we are carrying on a campaign of developing new and unusual ideas to improve and sell *Metropolitan News*. You have been invited to a brainstorm session on the problem:

> *How to increase our weekday morning circulation in the city.*"

Since the brainstorm session was to be held on Wednesday, Douglas told his secretary to distribute the invitations first thing Monday morning. Most of the members had brainstormed before, but those who hadn't received a mimeographed booklet which Douglas had prepared for them. He also wrote a note on their invitation asking them to come ten minutes early so that he could give them a briefing on brainstorming and answer any of their questions.

When Wednesday came, the first-timers met in the pine-paneled conference room where the brainstorm session was to be held. They came at ten minutes of twelve, and Douglas gave them a quick talk. At twelve the rest of the panel arrived, and Douglas took a seat, not at the head of the table, but down along one side. His secretary was also there, and she would act as secretary for the group. Douglas introduced everybody, and after a light lunch of consommé, shrimp-salad sandwiches, potato chips, fruit and coffee, during which everybody loosened up and got to know one another, the session began.

Fritz Dalton, the assistant circulation manager, came in and gave a quick rundown on the problem of selling a morning newspaper in the city. He explained that since World

War II many of the paper's readers had moved to the suburbs, and that in many cases their businesses had moved in the same direction. They drove to work and no longer passed through the train terminals and subway stations where they used to pick up the morning paper. He noted that when the papers had raised their price to a nickel, many readers who used to pick up all the morning papers chose only one. He added that a cut in commuter train service had meant that more people drove to work and therefore did not read a paper during the ride in. At the end of his talk, he left. Douglas ceremoniously placed the bells on the table which were to be rung if any killer phrases were mentioned, and to make sure everyone understood, he read a few: "It won't work." "Let's form a committee," at which there was laughter. "Production won't accept it," at which the production man chuckled and ducked his head. Then Douglas added another one after a pause, "The publisher's assistant won't like it," and everybody laughed with the publisher's assistant.

There was a short pause, and the sports writer started out, "Let's put out a coffee-break edition, sell it during the mid-morning break."

Then there was a hitch-hike, "Have those office caterers display it for sale."

"Have it printed napkin size."

"Print it in small type so it can be read in a short break."

"Don't sell it here; the publisher doesn't believe in the morning break."

"That's a killer phrase." Douglas roared and rang a bell.

Everyone laughed, and then the police reporter piped up, "We deliver the paper to hotel rooms, let's deliver it to offices."

"Have it delivered right to executives' desks."

"Sell it to their secretaries too."

One of the young advertising men piped up, "Have an ad tie-in with a coffee company. Plug their coffee for the morning break."

"Give an office catering company a break on their ads if they'll have their boys sell the paper."

"Run more stories for businesswomen."

"Promote the idea that it pays for the career woman to be informed."

"That the pay-off is more men." Laughter. It was the young secretary who had spoken.

"Women shoppers read the ads as much as news; make sure we have papers for them when they come in in midmorning. Plug the idea that they'll find better bargains if they read our papers on the way in."

"Run a series on how to pick a baby sitter."

Douglas broke in, "Good idea, but let's remember we are trying to sell the paper downtown today."

"There are a lot of schools downtown, not only colleges and public schools, but vocational and business schools. Make sure we have papers they can buy between classes."

"Page one stories that will appeal to them."

"And to businessmen."

There was a pause. Douglas didn't seem at all anxious. A couple of people looked uncomfortable, but the old-timers at brainstorming were relaxed. After a while Douglas came up with an idea he had obviously thought of to use in such a case, "Sell the paper at the big parking lots."

"Have paperboys cover the major points where cars get jammed up coming into town."

"Make hay while the traffic jams."

"Have our trucks create traffic jams." Laughter.

"Sell their papers by the truckload."

"Every driver a supersalesman."

"Every salesman a traffic jammer."

"Yeah, I remember one morning out at Brown Circle," one of the men started to say, "why, cars were backed up for three and a half miles. I could have read *War and Peace*. I got to work four hours late that day, and did old Max lay me out. . . ." Douglas cut in, "I've had the same problem, and used the same alibi other times too." There was laughter. "Let's remember we're trying to sell papers downtown. That was a good idea about trying to sell papers when the cars are backed up, though. We've got ten minutes to go, let's make the most of it."

"Let's put out a bulldog edition to sell to people after the theater."

"After the ball game, the fight."

"At the big drive-in movies; they get out late."

The brainstorm session went on. At the end of twenty-five minutes they had come up with seventy-two ideas. That afternoon Douglas's secretary typed up the list, and the next day she called each brainstorm member to ask them if they'd thought up any ideas since they left the meeting. Six had, and they added seventeen more to the list. Douglas threw in a couple more himself, and then the list was retyped.

The next morning he called Fritz Dalton up to his office, and the two of them went over the list. They quickly crossed out the ridiculous ones, such as the napkin-sized paper, eliminated those which had been tried, and others which were marginal cases. In a week seven new ideas had been put to work. Douglas had sent copies of the complete list to the brainstorm members; now he sent each of them a memo, thanking them for their time, congratulating them on their creativeness, and telling them that seven of their ideas, a mighty good return on the investment, were now at work. Then he pulled his yellow pad in front of him and started to plan another brainstorm on how to increase the circulation of the paper in the new exurbs out beyond the suburbs.

That's how a brainstorming session works. Now I've chosen several real brainstorm case histories so you can see that a brainstorm works in fact as well as in fiction.

First is a brainstorm run by Trans World Airlines, a concern which has been doing a great deal of creative thinking in a very competitive field.

The invitation below was sent out by Gerald R. Thornton, Assistant General Sales Manager and brainstorm chairman, to panel members. The fourteen members included the advertising director, an advertising agency vice-president, two TWA vice-presidents, the director of customer relations, an executive secretary, assistant supervisor of hostesses. In all five women attended the luncheon session in a company conference room.

> *Thanks for agreeing to serve on the next Brainstorm panel May 31. We will get together at noon in the conference room for lunch and should finish by 2 P.M.*
>
> *The question to be brainstormed is "What changes would you make in the TWA timetable?"*

We want to consider changes in format, use, size, shape, design, or any change that would make the time-table a better sales tool for TWA.

Some changes were made in April, including new typography and additional condensed schedules. What other constructive changes would you recommend?

About ten issues of the timetable are printed each year in order to keep schedule information up to date. About 200,000 copies per month are used in our own offices and in flight packets on our planes. From 125,000 to 200,000 of each issue are mailed to important accounts, travel agents, and other airlines.

Attached is a copy of the June 1 timetable.

To those ten of the fourteen who were attending their first brainstorm he attached the following P.S.

Since this is the first time you have served on a Brain-storm panel, I am attaching some information on the sub-ject. You should read it over before our meeting so you will understand the brainstorming technique.

When the list was copied after the brainstorm he sent out the following note to each member—with the unorganized list of the ideas just as they fell in the session.

Thank you for participating in our Brainstorm session on Thursday. You can all feel very pleased at the large number of ideas produced!

The full list of 152 ideas is attached. You will notice that all hitch-hike ideas are preceded by the symbol "HH" and directly follow the idea, or ideas, to which they are hitching. If you can think of any additional ideas, let me know within the next few days. We have already had several of these "after thoughts" and have incorporated them into the list.

A small committee will be meeting this week to condense this list to a few ideas that can be submitted to the Advertising Department. I will keep you advised of the final results.

Hope we can get together for another Brainstorm session soon!

This is a long transcription, but it is vital to include it because this is the only way you can see the brainstorm in action. This is the way fourteen persons reacted when faced with a problem and were allowed to speak without inhibition. This is the chain reaction—not in a classroom experiment, but in a real situation when a group of tough, practical businessmen sat down to solve a company problem.

1 *Map, page 15, show our routes in color—red.*

2 *Put map inside cover—not in center.*

3 *Use different color combination for cover—everybody has red and blue—use distinctive, different colors.*

4 *Change color each issue.*

5 *On cover, indicate timetable is effective from —— until —— so passenger knows whether he has latest timetable.*

6 *Back cover—show four or six months' worth of calendar (many bookings made far in advance).*

7 *HH—show four months—one current, three ahead—eliminate all advertising and give room for expense account and other notations.*

8 *Front cover—have testimonial and autograph of famous person—TWA traveler.*

9 *HH—have whole lot of autographs on front cover, all celebrities.*

10 *Have picture of globe on front cover.*

11 *Page 15—at base of maps show total mileage—both in U.S. and Europe.*

12 *Front cover—reverse logo—red on white for better legibility.*

13 *Cheesecake on front cover.*

14 *HH—have picture on light side.*

15 *Print map in back.*

16 *HH—print map on back cover.*

17 *Front picture of TWA service—hostess, reservations agent, ticket agent, etc.*

18 *Front picture—a number of top TWA executives—between them, they have —— years of service and experience.*

19 *HH—captains.*

20 *HH—hostesses.*

21 *HH—and hostesses' telephone numbers.*

22 *HH—airplane pictures.*

23 *Front picture—plane flying over the clouds.*

24 *HH—horizontal picture.*

25 *HH—under clouds put "100 flights per week to Europe."*

26 *Off-season—front picture of Marilyn Monroe in a Sleeper Seat.*

27 *Advertise we are only carrier with both U.S. and Europe, and through service.*

28 *HH—show on front cover that we operate both domestically and overseas.*

29 *Eliminate term, "Domestic"—use rather, "U.S."*

30 *Plug travel agents.*

31 *HH—big agents who use a lot of timetables—have their names imprinted.*

32 *Fold timetables the other way—flip more easily to page desired.*

33 *Call attention to* new improved *timetable, or* new handy timetable.

34 *For women—to fit better in purse—smaller edition, about two inches shorter than present timetable.*

35 *HH—perfumed timetables for women.*

36 *HH—timetable to be tied with pink ribbon instead of stapled.*

37 *Have every page perforated for easy removal—segment timetables only to be printed.*

38 *HH—perforate pages of condensed schedules for easy removal.*

39 *HH—put these in pads—all page 1, or page 2, etc.*

40 *Have small timetable—and little counter rack similar to Mary Gordon leaflet rack.*

41 *HH—have small timetable showing* only that flight segment *on overseas flights (show* IDLPAR *on* IDLCAI *flight for those only going to Paris).*

42 *Condensed schedules, all segments, east and westbound.*

43 *HH—segments to show two cities only* (not PHL-PIT-CHI *etc.*).

44 *HH—individual timetables, segments, for major stations —no fares shown.*

45 *Keep all condensed segments together, put page 14 with first 3 pages.*

46 *Have explanation on how to use timetable—condensed segments.*

47 *Domestic—eliminate "Condensed"—call them "Express" flights.*

48 *Eliminate separate Constellation schedules, pages 4 and 5.*

49 *Eliminate condensed schedules altogether.*

50 *Index—list cities, followed by page number where schedule is found. Also, page numbers to be bigger.*

51 *More pictures of planes—have Connie pointing to page numbers.*

52 *Right inside fold—table of contents—make more readable, show subject and page in two columns.*

53 *Eliminate table of contents.*

54 *Let "L" stand for lunch—corresponding symbols to apply for other meals.*

55 *Bottom of page—symbol for meals to be crossed fork and knife, cup and saucer for snack, etc.*

56 *HH—all references, footnotes, to be consolidated in one place only.*

57 *Page 13—eliminate footnote "g."*

58 *Make up separate domestic and international timetables.*

59 *Have separate section for tourist and first class.*

60 *List all tourist flights together and all first class flights.*

61 *HH—show multiple service in both tourist and first class sections.*

62 *Have separate segmental schedules for three regions.*

63 *Keep flight departure time and flight number constant.*

64 *Keep directions consistent and not NYC-oriented (Domestic WB & EB, International WB & EB).*

65 *Number flights in more logical fashion.*

66 *Use low numbers for flights—start with 1 and 2 and keep them low.*

67 *Arrange major common destinations on even and consistent hours (all PIT flights at quarter past the hour, all LAX flights on the hour, etc.).*

68 *Show statistics—how many 1049s we now have, what our goal in number of 707s is, etc.*

69 *Publish by service, first class or tourist—include "from" and "to" and fares.*

70 *Use logical wording—"Leave* NYC—LGA."

71 *List International Airport first to eliminate emotional block of considering* IDL *as further away than* LGA.

72 *Print plane plan and seat numbers for passengers' choice of seats.*

73 *On International schedules eliminate Note D showing plus or minus how many hours.*

74 *Domestic—eliminate connecting flights—look like "bug tracks."*

75 *HH—for greater legibility, especially with little light, print in black and white.*

76 *HH—print westbound schedules in left-hand fold.*

77 *Do more to distinguish between* A.M. *and* P.M.

78 *HH—print* A.M. *and* P.M. *in red and blue for contrast.*

79 *Eliminate little dashes for cities where flights do not stop.*

80 *If room, indicate state after cities—two- or three-letter code.*

81 *HH—print name of country after city.*

82 *HH—for twin cities, show which one we land at.*

83 *HH—print city names all in caps with first letter larger.*

84 *HH—indent cities after first of each section listed.*

85 *HH—treat domestic schedule like international—with everything printed bigger.*

86 *Print Ambassador symbol (top hat, gloves, and cane) at heading of each Ambassador flight.*

87 *Eliminate shading of Sky Tourist column.*

88 *Shade columns for tourist flights on domestic as now done on international.*

89 *Eliminate shading in* ALL *tourist flight columns.*

90 *Use color designations for Gs, perhaps also 1049s (possibly all first class).*

91 *At top of column, indicate type of equipment in words—Constellation, Martin.*

92 *Indicate flying time between stations.*

93 *Eliminate "Eastbound" and "Westbound" captions on timetables—confusing for small hops in midwest.*

94 *Page 14—eliminate bargain air freight.*

95 *HH—eliminate all page 14 schedules,* YIP, CVG, *etc., too local.*

96 *With air freight schedule, indicate cost.*

97 *HH—indicate cost of air parcel post and air express.*

98 *HH—have one whole page on air freight, etc.*

99 *Pages 16 and 18—eliminate all connections with Ethiopian.*

100 *HH—show connecting schedules to more popular off-line points.*

101 *HH—show connections in condensed schedules on page 3.*

102 *Eliminate type of schedule as exemplified by pages 4–13, have only box segment type.*

103 *Page 17, box—show connection time to* EWR *too.*

104 *Show helicopter connections at* LAX, NYC, *etc.*

105 *HH—include helicopter connections to* EWR, LGA, IDL.

106 *Page 14, eliminate schedule for* NYC *to* HOU *via Memphis, Shreveport, etc.*

107 *Eliminate italics on connecting flights (like San Diego and Baltimore) confusing.*

108 *Page 3—*NYC, CHI, PHX, LAS *indications misleading.*

109 *Don't print once-a-week flight in condensed schedules—misleading.*

110 *Page 21—International offices, cut out repetitions (Paris four times, London twice).*

111 *Page 21—eliminate International sales information—unnecessary columns, such as name of District Sales Manager, etc.*

112 *HH—pages 20 and 21, eliminate all off-line ticket offices —leave more room for vital information.*

113 *Page 20, left side, eliminate cable address, auto rental, etc.*

114 *Eliminate last six columns page 20 domestic information (ticket office, ticket office hours, airport miles from city, city to airport transportation time, fare inc. gov. tax).*

115 *Pages 22 and 23—clarify Domestic and International for General Passenger Information, misleading as stands, looks like 22 is domestic and 23 international.*

116 *HH—General Passenger Information should be streamlined into one half the present words.*

117 *Page 22—rehead: "Helpful passenger information" or "Timesaving passenger information."*

118 *Pages 18 and 19, stress international and domestic connections.*

119 *Pages 22 and 23, eliminate "in U.S. currency" and dollar signs—this is domestic schedule.*

120 *Indicate more clearly that ticket office hours are not same as reservations hours—reservations usually open 24 hours.*

121 *HH—print columns for office hours and telephone reservations closer together.*

122 *Page 23, Fares—print fares in two colors to distinguish more readily between tourist and first class.*

123 *With fares—explain Time Pay Plan.*

124 *Have something light—anecdote, cartoon, each issue.*

125 *Each issue, have limerick, advertising* TWA, *to be com-*

pleted, entry blank in flight packet on plane. Advertise and announce last timetable's winner.

126 *Sell advertising in timetables.*

127 *Print four-color wrapper and four-color center section.*

128 *Put more emphasis on baggage allowance and restrictions.*

129 *HH—print timetable so that it unfolds to tape measure and indication of how large carry-on luggage may be.*

130 *HH—cartoon showing overburdened passenger with $$$ signs (excess baggage charge).*

131 *Mailing—have dignified, first class envelope, marked* PERSONAL.

132 *HH—have envelope of thick enough paper that timetable doesn't shine through.*

133 *HH—show photo of Super G on back of envelope.*

134 *HH—no envelope; address on timetable.*

135 *HH—use cellophane envelopes.*

136 *HH—use envelope to promote current features—Sleeper Seat, Family Plan, Time Pay, etc.*

137 *Include coupon to send in for Skyliner Tours and Mary Gordon leaflets.*

138 *HH—send names of friends.*

139 *HH—passengers' names to be put on mailing list.*

140 *HH—explanation of* ATP.

141 *HH—coupon for hostess applicants.*

142 *HH—rotate above five inserts.*

143 *"If you please" letter to Collings—insert in timetable.*

144 *Feature a different noncompetitive interline carrier each month.*

145 *Limit distribution of large timetables to ticketed passengers.*

146 Issue only seasonal timetables—have changes picked up by Reservations.

147 Name flights.

148 HH—more names—like "Royal Coachman," names by class of service, or nonstops, etc.

149 When this list of improvements has been screened, have board of outsiders (ATP accounts, other frequent users, and seasoned travelers) advise whether final suggestions really are practical. This to be done only twice a year or so.

150 HH—have secretaries of important businessmen give their ideas on timetable improvements (perhaps prize for best suggestions).

151 Make timetable easy to read.

152 Activate everything next month.

A screening committee boiled that list down to sixty-two ideas. Many of the ideas on that screened list were put to use, and the new table was startlingly improved. It was more attractive; it gave the customer more information more easily than the old one; it carried out the airline's advertised promise of service; in short, the brainstorm session did accomplish its mission: it made the timetable a strong TWA selling point.

One of the most progressive—and successful—banks in the United States is the Valley National Bank of Phoenix, Arizona, which today ranks sixty-second among the nation's fifteen thousand commercial banks. This bank so thoroughly serves the citizens of its state that it has, statistically, a customer in every Arizona family. Its astonishing growth is due in part to the creative way it has served its customers. Brainstorming is a part of their operating technique. To those who think brainstorming a Madison Avenue thing, not at all applicable to the world of profit and loss, investment and finance, here are some examples of what can be done in the staid old business of banking.

The person in charge of brainstorming at the Valley National Bank is Mrs. Mildred F. May, assistant cashier and director of Special Service. "Although you will see how many ideas have been put to work in each session," Mrs. May wrote me, "frankly, there were so many good practical ideas advanced that we rather suffer from an embarrassment of riches and have not yet had time to put them all into effect."

The invitation was sent out by the chairman, H. L. Dunham, Vice-Chairman of the Board. Twelve people attended the 8:30 A.M. session. They included three assistant cashiers, an advertising department member, an administrative assistant, a secretary, a vice-president, an assistant vice-president, a member of the relief staff, and manager of the stenographic pool. There were nine women and three men. They discussed the problem of "Savings Deposits . . . how can we hold on to what we have . . . how can we increase the deposit activity of our customers . . . how can we attract new accounts?"

They came up with fifty-eight ideas and put six to work. Those ranged from making the final coupon in an installment loan payment book a signature card to open a savings account, to buying a supply of lollipops to give away to youngsters so they would be happy and quiet while their parents did business with the bank.

Another time a Valley National brainstorm was called by the vice-chairman of the board and held in his office. On this occasion ten persons attended, all men. They included three assistant vice-presidents, the advertising director, a trust officer, a vice-president, and two branch managers.

The problem they attacked was a jawbreaker: "How can we better capitalize upon the expenditures we make during the period of preparation for a branch opening and the actual open-house date, by continuing to maintain the high level of good will and accounts first opened during the period of the first ninety days, six months, one year?"

They did come up with forty ideas, however, and put fourteen to work. These included opening accounts right at the open house, developing a specialized new business staff for residential areas, putting up directional signs to lead people to branches which were not on main intersections, and putting rest rooms on the main floor. They also suggested holding a brainstorm with branch managers before planning the layout of new branches.

They did that with good results, and here's the case history on that brainstorm which grew out of a brainstorm.

Notice that Mr. Dunham shifted the locale of the brainstorm and used a warm-up technique. This time nine persons attended, seven of them branch managers, and again all men.

Quite a few of our managers have indicated an interest in having a "Brainstorming" session on the layout and physical aspects of new branches.

Most of you have been through these sessions before, so we won't go into the ground rules, etc.

To add a little immediacy to this meeting, we will hold it at the spanking new 16th Street and Camelback office here in Phoenix, at 8:30 A.M., Thursday, April 26.

This will also give Dale the opportunity to face all of his "severest" critics at once.

Remember, this meeting is your opportunity to bring out your wildest ideas and dreams on this subject—so empty out that "drawerful" of gripes and suggest the answers as ideas.

The subject will probably be stated as, "If you were responsible for laying out and designing the interiors of new branches, what changes would you make, what additions, what deletions?"

See you BRIGHT AND EARLY!

This is the report Mr. Dunham sent out to brainstorm members:

This meeting, except for short flurries of activity, was not a true "Brainstorming" session—but as a combination of "Brainstorming" and prelisted ideas it accomplished the purpose. You managers were on a subject so close to your hearts that you arrived too well prepared for a straight "new idea" session.

The results of the meeting, as you will find in the reading, were excellent.

For the benefit of the evaluators we have broken your "suggestions" into five categories.

I   *Interior Layout*
II   *Interior Space Requirements*
III   *Furnishings, equipment, and appearance*
IV   *Exterior*
V   *Miscellaneous*

Of course, we had the ten-minute warm-up session on Valley Bank anniversaries, which we have recorded for your benefit also. All in all, you fellows produced a whale of a lot of suggestions in the time allotted.

We will probably be calling on you again soon on the matter of a "New Managers Check List."

VALLEY BANK ANNIVERSARIES (*Warm-up*)

1 *Let branches handle their own anniversaries.*
2 *Separate the ten-year anniversary and up group from those under.*
3 *Keep our present setup but change time to evening.*
4 *Have each celebrant give a little personal history at the meal.*
5 *Keep the branches coming to the luncheon.*
6 *Extend our present deal and get as many more branches in it as we possibly can.*
7 *Include a tour of Home Office and possibly a branch or two in the anniversary deal.*
8 *Have bank pay for the meal.*
9 *Make the meeting semimonthly to break up the size.*
10 *Definitely continue the letters—very effective.*
11 *Make a program of it—including a welcoming address from management.*
12 *Give something besides a cake; perhaps perfume for one year (girls) etc. Something that connotes anniversary and lasts.*
13 *Have anniversary luncheons on an individual basis with immediate supervisor and a guest.*
14 *Send out pictures for the bulletin board in each office represented.*
15 *Develop an anniversary album for each office (and department?).*
16 *Invite all participants from all the branches in the valley area to an evening affair.*

17 Include wives and husbands.
18 Give a gift to the husband or wife on the 25th anniversary.
19 Discontinue anniversaries altogether.

It was also recommended that we write a letter to families asking if they would be interested in attending an annual affair to hear talks from management and witness awards, etc.

Then we started on the five main subjects.

I INTERIOR LAYOUT

1 Work out a system to store supplies right next to the operations people that use them. Use bookcase shelves or cabinets for neat and colorful stacking. Farmers & Stockmen use in their bookkeeping department.

2 Put both men's and women's rest rooms on main floor.

3 Have drive-in windows as close as possible to tellers for convenience in reliefs, etc.

4 Keep new accounts and operating departments closer together.

5 Take new-accounts department away from officers' rail— give more privacy.

6 Make sure the note cage has an entrance beside one into (and through) officers' quarters.

7 Never isolate the drive-in window (example in Chandler).

8 Build vaults in front end of bank, better for tellers and customers.

9 Have a community room in all banks.

10 Make sure the supply room and book vault are all on the same floor.

11 Separate the new-accounts area completely from loaning area.

12 *Design the bank to eliminate traffic behind tellers' cages. Route through work spaces instead of through tellers' cages.*

13 *Partition off the new a/c area.*

14 *Provide a sit-down area for new accounts, especially for waiting.*

II INTERIOR SPACE REQUIREMENTS

15 *Provide larger work area for mail desk.*

16 *Provide larger officers' area for expansion. (East Van Buren, 24th & Thomas, 16th & Camelback, West Van Buren, bad examples).*

17 *If necessary, move boiler and refrigeration equipment upstairs.*

18 *Put more shelving in the stockroom.*

19 *Provide more counter and work space in tellers' cages.*

20 *Stockroom shelving should be spaced wider—perhaps use flexible, movable shelving. Presently very difficult to get record boxes (cartons) out of shelves.*

21 *Generally double workroom space over what has been planned in the past. We set up for tellers' expansion—but do not plan for work space to keep up with tellers.*

22 *Provide this additional space on a measured-out basis.*

23 *All of these man-saving procedures inevitably seem to take more room for equipment.*

24 *Need more customer desk space.*

25 *Provide more work space on the new a/c counter. Deeper than others.*

26 *Make provisions to make new a/c customer just as comfortable as a loan applicant.*

27 *Provide more ample rail space for opening new a/c.*

28 *Make lower, conference-top counters for sit-down convenience at new a/c rail.*

III FURNISHINGS, EQUIPMENT, AND APPEARANCE

29 *Provide more adequate signs.*

30 *Put a partition or wall between tellers and bookkeepers.*

31 *All gates should swing both ways.*

32 *Have better plastered walls so that enamel paints may be used if and where desired.*

33 *Provide drinking fountain for children.*

34 *Put a partial partition around the drive-in window (inside) for noise protection.*

35 *Put rubber treads on stair steps.*

36 *Warmer-appearing conference room.*

37 *Provide wider entrances to cages to accommodate trucks.*

38 *Provide more than one control for sound system so adjustment (volume) can be made in specific areas.*

39 *Supply storage rooms with small truck for carting supplies around the bank.*

40 *Spend more time planning electrical and telephone outlets. Provide both as twins wherever possible.*

41 *Provide just double the number of electrical sockets now installed.*

42 *When partitioning off bookkeeping area, provide a transparent top at least in the officers' area to make a showplace of operations. This segment of the partition could even come out obliquely from the side wall for visibility from rail.*

IV EXTERIOR

43 *Provide walk-up tellers' windows.*

44 *Provide for more expansion.*

45 *Immediately put in underground sprinkler system whenever grass is planned.*

46 *Shade the drive-in windows. Even the counter itself reflects the sun into the teller's eyes.*

47 *Provide the night depository with envelope chutes.*

48 *Put in more windows so the public can see in and out.*

49 *Get rid of those large fixed louvers that completely obstruct the view through the front of the bank.*

50 *More side-of-the-building parking—to be used for branch expansion later.*

51 *Make the exterior of the building as modern as the interior usually is.*

52 *Give more consideration to the traffic flow into and out of your drive-in window.*

53 *Install the air intake farther away from the incinerator exhaust.*

54 *Put a taller stack on the incinerator.*

55 *Put a desk at drive-in to hold customers' supplies (outside) and provide some base or platform for writing.*

56 *Provide more open approaches to drive-in windows so that people can keep from trapping themselves in a line of cars.*

57 *Keep banks to single floor.*

58 *Adopt a completely different style of building to reduce costs—a more functional building (even grocery-store type).*

V MISCELLANEOUS

59 *Get all equipment in bank before painting.*

60 *Set up a committee for new branch locations including branch managers for choosing sites.*

61 *Branch managers should see final plans on building.*

62 *Dropping construction costs on new buildings is not an answer—we should build a big front.*

63 *Start branches smaller—with better and larger expansion planned.*

64 *Have closer and more complete co-ordination between the final inspections and actual move-in. Work in full co-operation with the manager and staff.*

65 *Adopt a tougher attitude with the contractors. Let's schedule the operation for our convenience and efficiency—not just theirs.*

66 *Let's not rush the opening quite so fast.*

67 *Design offices for operation by a minimum crew—allowing for utilization of additional spaces as needed with growth.*

68 *A better and more complete analysis of microfilm records to relieve record storage problem.*

Out of a total of 87 ideas, 21 have been put to use. That's a return of 24 per cent on the bank's investment of time and effort, and that more than makes a very excellent bank quite happy. This is the bank's own result list:

IDEAS USED FROM SESSION

(WARM-UP)

5 (*Keep the branches coming to the luncheon.*) Done.

7 (*Include a tour of Home Office and possibly a branch or two in the anniversary deal.*) Tours of the Home Office now used.

8 (*Have bank pay for the meal.*) Bank is now paying for meal.

(ACTUAL SESSION)

1 (*Work out a system to store supplies right next to the operations people that use them. Use bookcase shelves or cabinets for neat and colorful stacking. Farmers & Stockmen use in their bookkeeping department.*) Now an integral part of all new plans.

2 Put both men's and women's rest rooms on main floor. Done wherever possible.

3 (*Have drive-in windows as close as possible to tellers for convenience in reliefs, etc.*) Followed except in exceptional cases.

8 (*Build vaults in front end of bank, better for tellers and customers.*) Doing this with few exceptions.

12 (*Design the bank to eliminate traffic behind tellers' cages. Route through work spaces instead of through tellers' cages.*) Part of all plans now.

15 (*Provide larger work area for mail desk.*) Implemented immediately.

16 (*Provide larger officers' area for expansion.*) Now routine.

22 (*Provide this additional space (i.e., workroom space) on a measured-out basis.*) Now routine.

34 (*Put a partial partition around the drive-in window (inside) for noise protection.*) Now routine.

36 (*Warmer-appearing conference room.*) Using interior decorators to accomplish.

38 (*Provide more than one control for sound system so adjustment (volume) can be made in specific areas.*) Now routine.

44 (*Provide for more expansion.*) Newest buildings all have expansion built in.

46 (*Shade the drive-in windows. Even the counter itself*

reflects the sun into the teller's eyes.) *Canopy now standard.*

49 (*Get rid of those large fixed louvers that completely obstruct the view through the front of the bank.*) *Eliminated use.*

51 (*Make the exterior of the building as modern as the interior usually is.*) *Trying with increasing success.*

57 (*Keep banks to single floor.*) *Becoming standard with rare exceptions when space necessitates.*

63 (*Start branches smaller—with better and larger expansion planned.*) *Definitely being practiced.*

66 (*Let's not rush the opening quite so fast.*) *Now delaying openings by intent; more time for last-minute details.*

EVALUATION PANEL:

H. L. DUNHAM, *Vice-Chairman of the Board*

LEGRANDE MOORE, *Vice-President, Properties Mgr.*

WILSON BARRETT, *Asst. V.P., Supervisor of Branches*

As you will notice, both of these brainstorms are vastly different from each other. They are also different in many ways from what I have described as the ideal way of running a brainstorm. But they did pay attention to Osborn's four basic rules—and they got results. That's the beauty of brainstorming. It is adaptable, and it produces under all sorts of conditions. In the next chapters we will show some of the ways it can be modified to cover many more situations than the classic company brainstorms we have been discussing.

SOLOS AND SMALL COMBOS

*how you
can brainstorm
by yourself*

*what equipment
you need*

*when and where
to solo brainstorm*

*how to stimulate
your subconscious*

*how to ignite
a solo
chain reaction*

*problems
for the solo
brainstorm*

*how small groups
brainstorm*

*the quick,
on-the-spot brainstorm*

*what one company
has done*

variations on a theme

The loudest argument people use to fight brainstorming is
that it is a group activity which needs twelve people. Oppo-
nents of the technique point out that man, even organization
man, is essentially a lonely animal.

They are absolutely right. No matter how many conferences a sales manager has to attend, he spends much more
time by himself. The same thing is true of the medical ad-
ministrator, the teacher, the engineer.

The average executive, committee-bound as he may feel,
rarely spends more than 10 per cent of his time in meetings.
And since few committees accomplish much except to con-
firm what has already been done, it is obvious that most
ideas come to people when they are alone; most problems
are solved by a lonely individual staring at a drawing board
or out a window. In fact, just about every final decision is
reached by one man alone—even if it is kicked around in a
hundred conferences and confirmed by a dozen committees.

Therefore, this is a most pertinent question about brainstorming: Can I use it during the 90 per cent of the time I
work alone?

The answer: An unqualified yes.

I have developed, tested, and practiced solo brainstorming that can just as effectively increase the creativity of individuals as group brainstorming can stimulate originality in
groups.

The solo brainstormer adapts the same basic rule—no negative thoughts—as the brainstorm panel. Since he obviously does not have to get twelve busy people together, he has almost complete mobility. All he has to have is a pencil and what I call an idea trap—some sort of paper which will preserve the fleeting, but practical, ideas produced by solo brainstorming. The idea trap can be a pocket notebook, a legal-size sheet of paper, a clip board, a desk pad, the back of an envelope, a three-by-five-inch card—anything that can be tucked away and saved until there is time to apply judgment to the ideas.

As in the group brainstorm, the first step is to pick a good question—a spade question that will produce specific answers.

Once that is done, I like to have my secretary hold off all calls and callers for a brief period of time—five, ten, or fifteen minutes—while I brainstorm. If that isn't easy, I slip off to an empty conference room.

I take a legal pad of paper, a pen and, as fast as I can, write down any ideas which come into my head on the problem under attack. Surprisingly enough most of us have negative thinking so well built into our system that it is easy to think killer phrases. Then we have to ring a bell mentally on ourselves. We do seem just as anxious to hide silly ideas, even if no one is ever going to see our list. Solo brainstorming takes some discipline, just as group brainstorming. We have to learn to free-wheel, but if we do, it is amazing what the subconscious can produce.

Many times you will find that you have been carrying in your head solutions to problems that logic wouldn't let you express, even to yourself. While you were looking at the problem in the proper, professional way, your subconscious was having its own offbeat and often brilliant ideas. Once you have them down on paper your professional background can make the difference by turning them into profits.

Solo brainstorming can be carried on anywhere. Many commuters find that they can brainstorm a problem they will face during the day on their way to work. Some men who travel a great deal brainstorm in the air—or in the club car. Some brainstorm how best to use the time they'll "waste" traveling and come up with some problem, you guessed it, to brainstorm. Many executives brainstorm before getting out of bed in the morning, especially if they've thought about the problem before going to sleep and let their subconscious puzzle over it while they snored. Others like to brainstorm just before they turn off the light at night when their subconscious is crowded with the impressions from a busy day.

Obviously a solo brainstorm lacks the stimulation of many minds. There are ways to beat this, however, which can easily be applied to any job.

If the problem to be solved involves something small and tangible—a package for frozen fish sticks, a new casting for an engine, the sole of a shoe—it's helpful to handle the object, looking at it from every different angle, holding it upside down, sidewise, turning it around in your hands. You might take different materials and apply your other senses to them. Depending on the goods, you might cut it, tear it, try to bend it, run your hand over it, even bite or smell it. The thing to do is to look at an old problem in a new way. Then as you get a new idea, no matter how screwy, write it down.

You can stimulate your own brainstorms in a hundred ways. A toy manufacturer brainstorms by parking his car beside a playground and watching children at play. A production boss walks along an assembly line, notebook in hand, noting down every idea that occurs to him.

Thumbing through magazines, the indices of technical journals, a catalogue of parts can be stimulating if it bears a relationship to your problem. For example, a chemist might ignite ideas by glancing through a list of chemicals offered by a supply house. While he did it his subconscious might hook up combinations of chemicals he would never have thought of logically.

A writer I know gets ideas by wandering through a library, haphazardly walking from section to section, looking at titles, idly flipping open books, hitting on ideas almost by chance.

A sales manager can brainstorm by strolling through a busy supermarket or department store; an architect by driving slowly past many homes; a city planner by flying over his home town in a helicopter.

One way to brainstorm drugstore displays, for example, is to drop into a dozen drugstores, chat with the owners about what displays they use and why—and then sit in the car and note down any ideas you get, either from talking with the druggist, from seeing competitors' displays, or just by seeing a drugstore in a new light.

To be an effective solo brainstormer you might keep books or pamphlets handy which stimulate you. We all have certain books or people who stimulate us. We might call up a friend who is stimulating to us, have him out for a drink or lunch, talk with him about the problem, or other things. You won't solve the problem then, but time after time you'll have good ideas after leaving him.

Books and pamphlets which stimulate new thoughts run the gamut of everything published. They might be technical books in your field; it might be the Bible, Thoreau's "Walden", or poetry. It might be *Iron Age,* Ogden Nash, or even the lecture notes you took in Professor Doriot's class twenty years before.

Sometimes we need to see our problems simply, and this can be done by going back to basic textbooks or even books written for children about our subject. You may be a graduate engineer with fifteen years' experience building bridges, but just because of that fact you may have lost the simple essentials in your professional awareness of all the details of your profession.

A lunch hour in an art museum, especially one devoted to modern works, can make you see color and shape in new and wonderful ways. The same way, a phonograph record can make you hear differently.

One of the most basic rules of creative thinking is observation. We all have to see to give impressions to our subconscious. Whenever possible we should brainstorm by seeing our problem in a new and simple way, not as a professional sees it, but as a visitor might if he came from Mars.

There are practically no limits to the subjects which can be brainstormed, and this is especially true of the solo brainstorm.

You can brainstorm important decisions in your career:

What to give your wife for her birthday.
What to cook your husband for anniversary dinner.
How to sell more of your product.
What you want in the new home you're building.

How to sell your old home.
Where to find money to start your own company.
How to ask the boss for a raise.
How to answer a difficult letter.
How to raise money for the new church.
Where to go on your vacation.
How to file articles from the medical journals.
What college to attend.
How to propose to your gal friend.
Where to find a new job.

After you have brainstormed your problem, have a cold water session. Wait a day or so, then quickly run down the list, crossing off ideas that are no good and underlining the ones to put to work.

Sometimes it is a good idea to file these lists so that you can refer to them: (1) to jog yourself into acting on them; (2) to use when you hit the same or similar problems later.

In every case it is a good idea to check up on yourself, to force yourself to act. You might note the ideas you intend to act upon on paper and tape it to the inside of your desk drawer so you see it every day, or in your sock drawer so you see it every morning. The list might be pasted to the mirror you use when shaving, on the other side of the sunshade in the car, inside your brief case, or stuck in the back of a book you are reading. Some men have their wives or secretaries send them the list through the mail in a week or a month. No matter how you do it, there should be some way to put pressure on yourself to do something about the ideas you have from a brainstorm.

You won't be an idea man until you've done something

with your ideas. But if you practice solo brainstorming you'll have ideas, new ideas, on hundreds of problems you've never been able to lick before, and they will be ideas which will make a difference in your life.

Just as brainstorming can be used by one person as well as the classic dozen, so it works miracles for two or three people in the office.

There's rarely any need for formal invitation. When two or three people are together working on a problem, one may suggest, "Let's brainstorm it." That's all that's needed. One member picks up a pencil and paper; the brainstorm begins.

Sometimes an assistant will regularly brainstorm with his boss on the problems ahead during the day. Other executives make it a habit to have a quick telephone brainstorm when they hit a snag on a problem. A conference hook-up can easily be arranged with the telephone company, and this is especially valuable when the sales manager in the New York office needs to brainstorm a problem with the production boss in the Ohio plant and the design engineer of a supplier hundreds of miles away from each of them.

The time, place, or the number of people is not vital. The important thing is that the subconscious is made to attack the problem with minimum difficulty and maximum effectiveness. It can produce amazing results with little damage to the day's schedule.

A team of three advertising men, for example, can brainstorm an idea—how can we use the morning's news on plastics to sell our campaign? This brainstorm can be held in the taxi on the way to the presentation—and the cab driver might come up with an idea too.

Some executives will brainstorm with their secretaries to get a woman's idea on a problem. Others contact a special customer or two, a foreman on the line with years of experience, a young assistant who is new to the business but loaded with ideas.

One company which has done astonishing things with the small brainstorm group is the Reynolds Metals Company. Under the direction of Cloyd Steinmetz, the live-wire director of sales training, creative thinking has been made an integral part of their operation.

For hard-headed, practical results listen to this: Summer was an aluminum slump period. Reynolds applied creative thinking to the problem; brainstorming played a leading role, and they came up with hundreds of ideas—their barbecue kit, foil cookbooks, and so forth. In three years summer became the peak period, and they started to brainstorm ways to boost winter sales.

Recently a division manager, an experienced salesman, and a new one called on a supermarket owner and tried to sell him Reynolds' seventy-five-foot economy roll of foil. They had all their statistics down pat, their arguments worked out. They made a classic presentation. He wasn't sold. He refused to carry the item.

Instead of going out and griping, they had a three-man, on-the-spot brainstorm session, and the youngest member came up with an idea.

That night they called on the owner and presented him with a bottle of his favorite wrapped in the economy roll in such a way that he had to unroll all the aluminum to get to the whisky. He unrolled foot after foot, and when he had sixty-seven and a half feet, this was scrawled in huge letters on the foil: "This last twelve and a half feet the housewife gets free when she buys the economy roll in your store." When he got to the bottle he said, "Sit down, boys, and let's open the bottle." He bought the economy roll.

Another salesman couldn't sell the aluminum package of cake mix Reynolds was pushing in a pineapple upside-down cake promotion. He went home and brainstormed the problem and came up with a screwy idea. He baked an upside-down cake himself and then, dressed in his wife's apron, drove the cake, piping hot, down to the store and served it to the sales manager and some customers. He got the sale, and the sales manager wrote the head of his company. The result, the item was sold to the whole nation-wide chain.

In Reynolds' Los Angeles packaging division office, for example, they couldn't have a "classic dozen" brainstorm. They have only five men. Instead they have a regular weekly five-man brainstorm session. Each week, in rotation, one of the men picks his toughest sales prospect, and all five brainstorm how to sell him. This has boosted sales in that area enormously.

Brainstorming is a part of every Reynolds sales meeting, and the men who come in off the road have contributed literally hundreds of usable, sale-producing ideas to every Reynolds division.

One of the best things about a small brainstorm is that it has none of the inhibiting factors of a big meeting. It can be casual and bring together people of all levels and ages, white collar and blue collar, without difficulty.

In the shop a foreman, design engineer, and a machinist

can brainstorm a new way to produce a product as they stand around the machine that will have to do the job. When a production line grinds to a halt, the breakdown can be brainstormed on the spot.

At Hotpoint in Chicago, a plant superintendent and two general foremen were turned down after they requested a $200,000 conveyor system. The three didn't cry in their beer; they sat down and brainstormed the problem. The result was an equally efficient system. Price? Only $4000.

Andrew R. Barr, Supervisor of the Esso Standard Oil Company's New York Division repair shop, gets a handful of mechanics together during a coffee break when he runs into problems. They stand around the problem in question —recently one was on how to reach an unloading valve in a difficult spot with a wrench. The problem was solved before the coffee was finished, by an idea of using a different wrench in an unconventional way. That's typical of what can be done.

Try it yourself. Brainstorm with your boss, your secretary, associates, assistant. Make it a regular part of your work day, and you'll be amazed how easily it will solve problems and produce valuable ideas.

IT COMES KING SIZE, TOO

*why members
of large groups
don't contribute ideas*

*how you can make
each member
a brainstormer*

*how you can
collect ideas
from hundreds of people*

*sparking a conference
or convention*

*uses of
the mass
brainstorm*

a test case

One of America's most serious problems is that we are becoming a nation of spectators.

It is significant that our national pastime is baseball, in which only eighteen people play while thousands sit in the stands, millions more listen on radio and watch on television.

We tend to go to large schools where we listen to lectures, attend movies or plays, listen to concerts or phonograph records. We exalt the star, the prima donna, and deprecate our own efforts. The same thing is true in our business life. Too often we go along doing a routine job, just watching the important moves being made by others.

This is not only bad for the individual who has little chance to express himself, to grow and learn; it is incredibly bad for the country.

We used to be proud of our pioneer heritage, in which "rugged individualist" was not just a trite political phrase, but a prime necessity. Even in World War II our infantry rated as a prime war asset the leadership ability of privates who could and did take over when their officers were killed. This did not very often happen in the armies of our enemies.

Yet, by group living, by being spectators in life, we are wasting away this great natural resource at a time when we need it most.

We desperately need the ideas of everyone. We have vast problems of survival, and to solve them we must mobilize the brain power of all our citizens.

The trend toward sheeplike attendance of great masses of people at meetings of all kinds has been a matter of concern to many of the nation's forward thinkers.

They have watched people attending all sorts of gatherings, from sales conferences to religious conferences, people gathered to solve the smallest or the biggest problems of the world—and they have seen them sitting, row on row, contributing nothing from their own experience or intellects. Never do they get a chance to participate.

One of the most creative of the people deeply concerned with this problem is Don Phillips, President of Hillsdale College, Hillsdale, Michigan. He not only saw the problem, he analyzed it, and then came up with a solution which works. His analysis is worth reprinting, for before we brainstorm we must understand reasons why most people will not speak up in groups of all sizes from small committees to huge conventions.

FACTORS PREVENTING SELF-EXPRESSION IN GROUPS

I EARLY TRAINING HAS NOT ENCOURAGED DISCUSSION

A At home—*parental domination.* At church—*"Listen!"*
B At school—*"Speak when spoken to," "Answer teacher's questions!"*
C In community—*"Children should be seen and not heard!"*
D Enjoy listening—*no mental strain and seems to be proper member role.*
E Depend on experts, *leaders, parents, etc. More courteous to listen.*

F *Wait to get new or startling idea to compete favorably with others.*

G *"If I suggest anything, I'll be put on a committee."*

II IMPORTANCE OF PHYSICAL ENVIRONMENT NOT CONSIDERED

A *Room stuffy, too hot, too cold, poorly lighted.*

B *Seating arrangements formal or uncomfortable.*

C *Speaker separated from group—too far away, or platform or stage too high, or*

D *Members of group cannot see or cannot hear speaker.*

E *Room too large—feeling of "barniness."*

III LITTLE OR NO PREPARATION OF GROUP FOR DISCUSSION

A *No feeling of belonging.*

B *Poor choice of subject (1) "No interest in it"; (2) "Don't know enough about it to comment"; (3) too broad; or (4) untimely.*

C *Topic poorly handled; (1) speaker tells all—nothing left to discuss; (2) not challenging—creating passivity; (3) incomplete introduction to question; (4) no advance warning so no readiness nor preparation.*

D *Questions to group (1) poorly worded; (2) not heard; (3) patronizing.*

E *Feeling of futility; (1) subject doesn't lend itself to action; (2) from past experience, "nothing can or will be done anyway."*

F *Resistance to imposed program—"They never ask me what I want."*

IV DOMINATION BY OTHERS

A *Unskilled leader—offers little encouragement or opportunity.*
B *Monopolizing member—unaware of or unwilling to accept proper role.*
C *Expert—who creates dependence by being too expert.*
D *The "Brass"—in whose presence few people care to "stick their necks out." Difference in social, educational, or economic status is similar.*

V FEAR OF RIDICULE

A *Fear of taking a stand which may be unpopular to friends.*
B *Fear of deficiency in (1) grammar, (2) physical expression (stuttering, weak voice, etc.), (3) emotional control (temperament, blushing, shaky voice), (4) fluency, (5) general appearance.*
C *Fear of appearing stupid, or not using "correct" parliamentary procedure.*

VI GENERAL FEELING OF INFERIORITY

A *"I don't know much anyway—let the others talk."*
B *"Don't dare talk (1) in such a large place; (2) in front of so many people."*
C *"I can't say what I really mean when I'm on my feet."*
D *Fear of being contradicted and of inability to "hold my own" in argument.*
E *Fear of offending others.*
F *Fear of expressing what may be minority opinion.*

G *Fear of taking time when so little has been saved for discussion.*

To solve the problem of mass silence, he devised a system which he named "Discussion 66," but which others have referred to as Phillips 66. Under this system a large group is broken down into small committee sessions of six members, who discuss the problem under attack for six minutes. Then they contribute suggestions or questions. The important thing is that each individual feels much freer in the small group to take part. He is encouraged to participate; he is made to feel that he, as an individual, is important, that his ideas have value, that his word is needed.

That idea of Phillips 66 has been used successfully in hundreds of different ways, and it has been combined with brainstorming.

Don Phillips himself went to a Detroit manufacturing company to give a talk on creative thinking. He found about eighty people in one department, and to illustrate his talk he decided, on the spur of the moment, to have them break into small groups and brainstorm the problem of how to improve the eraser, since he had just been using one on the blackboard section of his talk.

They were allowed only six minutes, and the results were surprising. One suggestion from the first group was that the bottom of the eraser be made of sponge rubber to keep down the dust. Another came up with the idea of a disposable base. The next section asked, "Why couldn't it have a handle like a flatiron?" That gave another group the idea of shaping the eraser like an iron so you could erase just one letter with the point. Six minutes after Don Phillips had his spur-of-the-moment idea, he had a long list of practical suggestions about the simple old eraser. The ideas were so good, in fact, that an eraser designed on those principles has recently been put on the market.

I have experimented with this technique and had amazing results in many companies, at all sorts of conventions, and with the military in the Pentagon.

I have every other row of people stand up, turn around, and face the row behind them. Then I form groups of six. I have each group choose a chairman and secretary. I also have them pick a nickname—Pile-drivers, Tough Guys, Yankees, Rebels, Dead End Kids, anything they think up. This team system develops a competitive spirit that sure sparks ideas.

I keep the groups small and limit them to six to ten minutes. I have found the average group comes up with fifteen to twenty ideas in six minutes, but once I had one come up with fifty-two in only six minutes by using creative thinking and appointing two secretaries.

There is hardly a limit to how this mass brainstorm can be used. A company could have the members of its regular annual sales convention come up with ideas for new lines, better products, different advertisements and promotions, improved packaging, calling upon their daily experience in contacting customers on the road.

It is possible to mass brainstorm in a town meeting to find new ways of raising taxes—or building schools. The PTA can use it and so can the teachers' organization.

It can be used equally well by union and management,

Democrats and Republicans, professional societies and fraternal organizations. The important thing is that in each and every case it makes the participants not just spectators but contributors.

And we all respond to that treatment.

The Henry J. Kaiser Company had seven groups ranging from seven to eleven persons answer this question: "What methods of intercompany communications can be employed to create a greater understanding of all companies, each to the others, of their plans, objectives, and current activities?"

The question might be simplified, yet the answers were good in quality. And the total . . . 241.

Here are the categorized results of a six-minute mass brainstorm I ran. The question was: "How can we improve the New York Hospital Personnel Association?" The numbers in parentheses indicate duplicate answers. In all, the group came up with 143 ideas, of which 44 were duplicates. Among the 99 usable ideas I think there are ones you can use in your own lodge, club, company, or organization.

1 RESEARCH

Maintain a standing committee on salary information (2).
Publish the results of one project completed each year.
Compare functions with other personnel organizations.
Plan more active research (3).
Determine what members' needs are.

2 TRAINING—EDUCATION

Set up good educational programs and get them started (2).
Have more literature provided on our educational program.

Offer short courses (2).
Hold "problem" clinics.
Offer scholarships.
Have field trips to institutions (4).
Co-operate with industrial personnel groups (2).
Provide information for people entering the personnel field.
Work with schools of Hospital Administration.

3 MEMBERSHIP—NEW MEMBERS

Membership committee should improve welcoming and acquaintance procedure.
New members should be introduced faster.
Set up "Big Brother" movement in Association (3).
Have a system for identifying members.
Certificates of membership should be issued.

4 MEETINGS

Encourage group discussions (3).
Use "brainstorming" in problem areas (2).
Have more specialized meetings.
Work on common hospital problems (3).
Have less repetition of topics.
Have more informal interchange.
Discuss "how," not "what."
Hold sessions where members discuss new ideas.
Have smaller discussion groups at meetings.
Have more case discussions.
Hire speakers (2).
Have joint meetings with other groups.
Have specialists speak on different phases of personnel.
Hold luncheon or dinner meetings (3).

Have a cocktail hour.
Have coffee breaks at meetings (3).
Charge 25 cents for nonattendance at meetings.

5 COMMUNICATIONS

Circularize employee publications, handbooks, house organs, etc.
Strive for more publicity in hospital journals (2).
Prepare and circulate monthly information bulletin (2).
Exchange information in bulletin form with other hospital associations in country (2).
Publish annual review of year's activities.
Circulate articles by members.
Appoint Public Relations Committee to publicize Association's activities (2).
Issue minutes and get notices out quicker.
Set up a central file for the Association to provide material for new members (2).
Advertise personnel positions open in various hospitals.

6 ORGANIZATION

Assign each member to a committee (2).
Establish a guidance and placement service.
Employ a full-time secretary; establish an office.
Establish a consultant bureau (2).
Set up our own employment agency (2).
Affiliate with other personnel associations.
Increase dues.
Establish grievance committee.
Establish a "new ideas" department.

7 MISCELLANEOUS

Have evaluation of recruitment procedures and sources.

Plan recreational activities, parties, social activities (5).
Have greater interhospital contacts.
Standardize methods and procedures.
Set up referral policies.
Give awards to hospital personnel directors for unusual achievement.
Get more of our activities in concrete form for members.
Have our members represent us with different organizations.
Work in conjunction with other hospital departments.

Remember, the most important thing in every case of brainstorming is to get the participants to think without inhibition. They have to operate with a green light, no holds barred. When you get any group of people, no matter how large or small, to do that, you will find solutions to your problems coming in an avalanche.

TAKE IT HOME TO MAMA

*how you
can brainstorm
at home*

*a housewife uses
brainstorming*

the family brainstorm

*problems for
the breakfast-table
brainstorm*

*how to make
your home life
richer with
brainstorming*

One of the most important functions of brainstorming is to bring creative thinking right into our home, to make it a part of our daily living.

American life has undergone an astounding revolution in the past few years. We have tremendous mobility, far greater leisure time, a larger income, and many more facilities on which to spend it. We have even been unleashed from the social shackles of the past; our life is more casual, and our horizons far broader.

One of the most amazing facts of our world is the real strides we have made in leisure time. A generation ago we worked from sunup to sundown, or after, six days a week. We had little chance to do anything but eat, sleep, and work. The housewife had to wash diapers by hand, scrub floors, grind her own baby food. A woman's work was literally never done.

Today men are working not a forty-hour week, but a thirty-seven and a half hour week in many industries. Our wives can do up the laundry, run the vacuum, and have the house in good order in a few hours.

Tied directly in with this is an entirely new concept of family living, which *McCall's Magazine* has called "Togetherness." It's a good description. Men are doing women's work —cooking, cleaning, taking care of their children, and housewives are doing men's work—painting the house, driving the car, continuing their career. Notice the parties in your neighborhood. Fewer and fewer break up into men on one side of the room and women on the other. We are learning to know each other better, to share and work together a great deal more.

Still there is great unhappiness in our world. With all our wealth, our leisure time, our opportunities to share experiences we are often tense, unhappy, frustrated. The main reason, I believe, is that we do not know what to do with our freedom. We can make rich use of our time and cure our unhappiness only if we take full advantage of our opportunities. The best way to do that is to brainstorm our problem right in the family.

There are many good reasons for doing this.

Brainstorming creates a sense of participation by all members of the family. Grandma and Junior can have an equal opportunity to express themselves and to take part in the direction of family living. It gives the family an atmosphere in which Junior's bubbling enthusiasm, Grandma's experience, can each be an asset instead of something to be scorned.

Family plans should be made with brainstorms. They can be held around the Saturday breakfast table, for example, to decide what we will do this weekend. They can be held of an evening to make plans on how to fix up the house, the summer place, the patio.

Family gatherings can be planned with brainstorms. "Let's have a different Christmas." "What can we make in the shop evenings?" "How can we contribute a project to our church?" "What will that project be? How will we run it?" "How can we start a weekend business in the garage?"

There are many problems which lend themselves to the

family brainstorm. Bud wants to earn the money for a ja-lopy; a family brainstorm might give him a hundred money-making ideas.

Brainstorming can solve problems of family discipline when every other method has failed. After you have tried psychology, logic, salesmanship, deprivation, torture, and beating to cure a child of writing on the walls, screaming "no" at everything, running out in the street or tearing up books, try a brainstorm and see what new approaches you can come up with.

One family I know came up with a bunch of ideas when they tried to break their three-year-old boy of writing on the walls. They ranged all over the lot. Some of them are:

Hang a sign on him saying, "I am a bad boy."
Hang drawings he has done on drawing paper on the wall.
Draw ugly marks on his tummy with crayons when he marks up the wall.
Give him a desk with a huge pad of paper.
Paint walls and hose them down.
Beat him.

Brainstorming will help you find a way to get children to eat—or stop eating. It can solve problems of brotherly feuds, toilet-training, teen-age dates, the use of the family car.

Here's a quick brainstorm I ran with a group of parents on how to get children away from TV and interested in reading:

1 Pull plug in TV set.
2 Break up the set.
3 Set a definite time for looking at TV.
4 Arouse interest in books.
5 Acquire a bad horizontal tube.

6 *Reorient antenna in order to get bad reception.*

7 *Select book that has been seen on* TV.

8 *Set example by reading yourself.*

9 *Buy portable radio for children.*

10 *Evaluate* TV *programs.*

11 *Encourage visits to library.*

12 *Have the children make book reports.*

13 *Give money for movies.*

14 *Donate a* TV *to library.*

15 *More outdoor companionship with parents.*

16 *As a result of seeing* TV *story (say Robinson Crusoe) give children same book to read and do research on.*

17 *Start reading aloud to them when young.*

18 *Read them good books.*

19 *Make reading as convenient as* TV.

20 *Give them their own bookcase in room.*

21 *Give records for Hi-Fi.*

22 *Give subscriptions to children's magazines.*

23 *Select books suitable to age.*

24 *Get them interested in daily newspapers, even if only the comics.*

25 *Help them with their homework.*

26 *Select type of news they read.*

27 *Discuss with them the books they have read.*

28 *Have them read to you.*

29 *At* PTA *meeting have subject discussed with teachers— get teachers to recommend books.*

30 *Encourage group reading.*

31 *Buy them a good dictionary.*

32 *Always answer questions if you can.*

33 *Buy a good children's encyclopedia.*

34 *Institute games requiring the use of words and general knowledge.*

35 *Get local schools to have course in fast reading and good reading.*

36 *Have children checked physically—there may be some reason why they are unable to read.*

37 *In addition to their allowance, give them a fee for each good book that they read.*

Medical science with its wonders has presented society with a new and very difficult problem, that is the problem of our senior citizens. With our smaller houses, our labor-saving devices, there is little room and, more tragic, often little need for Grandma, and we all need to be needed. She feels in the way. Soon a major crisis can occur, a painful one from which every member of the family suffers.

A family might solve this problem through a brainstorm with Grandma participating. Here are some of the ideas that might come from such a session:

1 *Let Grandma shop and market for some of the meals.*

2 *How about letting it be her house weekends?*

3 *She could work as a volunteer in the hospital.*

4 *She could form a club for senior citizens and use the play-room for the meetings.*

5 *She could study art in the university extension.*

6 *She could become a teacher's helper at morning play school.*

7 *She could set up a neighborhood baby-sitting service.*

8 *We could have Grandma Week once a month, when she took charge running the house and the family.*

9 *She should take a monthly visit to the city.*

10 *Take the sight-seeing trips she has always dreamed about.*

11 *Take a friend with her.*

12 *Take one of the youngsters with her.*

13 *Taking care of one floor should be her job.*

14 *She could board pets.*

15 *She could be an answering service for the minister.*

16 *She could work with older folks in the church.*

17 *How about a church nursery?*

18 *She could sell her crocheting.*

19 *Teach it to Brownies.*

20 *Work a few hours in a store.*

21 *Learn to drive.*

22 *Have an attic sitting-room of her own.*

23 *Write a newspaper column for senior citizens.*

Brainstorming is a wonderful device for getting out of the rut of conventional living. The family could come up with new games to play in the evenings—a family ping-pong tournament or a neighborhood one. Reading projects in history or other subjects could be set up. How about a craft night at home? Ever think of taking walks? Get the architect across the street to show you the best in new homes or famous buildings on the walks. You might make weekend visits to a farm, a factory, a newspaper, churches of all denominations.

Get out of the eating rut. Have one member of the family besides Mother make one meal a week, Junior and Dad included. Have United Nations meals. Go to the library and get a cookbook and have a Japanese meal, a Turkish meal, a Spanish meal, a Southern meal, a New England meal. Ask students from the areas to share them with you. Invite somebody from the UN to spend their vacation in your home.

Let the ideas tumble out and see how your world grows and changes.

Families need ideas just as much as corporations, for ideas are the magic spices which make family life rich and full—and each member of the family a better and far happier person.

Brainstorming can and should be used to solve serious family problems, not only how to keep your wife from hanging nylons on your favorite gun rack, but also on how to keep your marriage together.

Every human institution has a number of problems and tensions which are built up and aggravated partially because of a breakdown in communications. The most basic human institution, the family, is no exception to the rule. Brainstorming can work to help solve the most intimate and difficult problems of marriage and family life.

The brainstorm is not only a way in which Junior can get off steam about his changing family status when he passes through the difficult teens; it can also be a way to help Dad get through the difficult forties, when the family seems to him in a swamp of routine living.

For example, in trying to find a subject to brainstorm, a man and wife who had been having their difficulties may realize that they haven't had a moment away from home without children, pets, friends, family, in-laws, or business associates underfoot. Then they can brainstorm such specific problems as: How to get time to go out on dates alone—where do we go and what shall we do—and therefore find a way to have a new marriage.

I firmly believe that any problem is well on the way to its

solution if it is first expressed and then defined. Brainstorming sessions can be a diplomatic way for both a man and his wife to express frustrations or grievances they have felt. And it is a constructive way. If the brainstorming rules are followed, the session should not break down into a spat. Remember, judgment is suspended during a brainstorm. If a man and wife can't brainstorm in the same room, they can each solo brainstorm the same problem in separate rooms and then exchange lists. Although if brainstorming alone saved such a marriage, it would indeed be a miracle.

Every human relationship has problems, and brainstorming is a tried and tested problem-solver. It can and should be used on the subtler problems of man and wife, father and son, mother and daughter, as well as the mechanical problem of how to make a better roller-bearing.

THE SHOE FITS, PUT IT ON

*how brainstorming
fits your business*

*examples of
brainstorming
used in many fields*

*a department-store
case history
of how it adapted
brainstorming
to special problems*

*how brainstorming
can work
in laboratories
and lodges,
union meetings, and
executive suites,
on the campus and
the production line,
in hospitals and
civic organizations*

a church case history

and one for travelers

When any new idea, such as brainstorming, comes along some of its most ardent disciples say it can be used in every situation to solve every problem. It can't. It is no cure-all; it won't bat 1000.

Brainstorming has, however, proved itself as a very dependable worker. It can produce an amazing assortment of solutions to a wide variety of problems. If it is used with thought, preparation and understanding, it is astonishing in how many widely different situations it can be employed.

Brainstorming will not be the same on Madison Avenue as it is on a Massachusetts campus. It will vary greatly when it is put to work in the Pentagon and in the Midwestern airplane factory, the medical center and the Hollywood film studio, the local lodge of Elks and the Republican Party.

There are few limits to brainstorming. Two or three elders can meet with their pastor for a moment after the Sunday service and brainstorm how to raise money to repair the roof or how to help the Eldridge family who have just suffered two bouts of polio and the loss of a job.

Neighbors can brainstorm ideas on how to decorate their yards or how to fight the zoning-board decision to let a factory move near their home. Two teen-age couples can brainstorm what to do after the Junior Hop.

Recently I saw three people brainstorm a way to dramatize a booth at a church meeting. In a few minutes they came up with many ideas. The one they used was to throw slides on the wall behind the booth rather than use the conventional banner or sign.

Columbia University brainstormed the question, "What will be the functions of the pharmacist in 1965 as a member of the health team?" They got 350 ideas on which to plan future courses.

Nationwide Insurance invited sixty-nine policy holders to Columbus, Ohio to brainstorm company problems.

I am going to quote extensively from a speech before a National Retail Dry Goods Association Sales Promotion Convention by Bob Cornelius, executive vice-president of Sattler's in Buffalo, New York. It's an amazing document. An early disciple of brainstorming and of Alex Osborn, he has made extraordinary use of brainstorming in his day-to-day work in a store far away from the shopping district, which has grown to a twenty-five million dollars a year business and had to have ten major additions in the past twenty years. Let him tell the story:

> *We have been using brainstorming at Sattler's for about twenty-one years. For many, many years we used it more or less secretly in the Advertising and Sales Promotion Division—secretly because we didn't want any brass in. That's one thing about brainstorming; if brass is in the room, brainstorming is no good. Unless it is all brass and they can brainstorm this thing among themselves.*
>
> *Now, in brainstorming a problem you really let yourselves go. Whatever occurs to you, you out with it. If it's dumb, silly, crazy, irrelevant, useless—that makes no difference. The point is, you may inspire the next guy across the table who thinks your idea is dumb—if he says*

so he will be run out of the brainstorming session—to come out with an idea that isn't dumb, but is workable and good. That is the history of our brainstorming sessions at Sattler's.

Sattler's is somewhat different from most stores in that we live on store traffic. We live on store traffic day by day. The telephone means nothing. They have to come into the store.

Now, we do a lot of things that a number of stores might consider beneath their dignity. We do it to bring people into the store. After we get them in there and expose our merchandise to them, they buy. But if we don't bring them into the store, we don't do business. So we have to continually dream up ideas to get hordes of people into the store.

We clock over a hundred thousand people in the store on many single days. When we quit clocking big crowds like that, we are going to quit being Sattler's.

We are located two miles from the downtown section. We have no theaters—we have one sort of scratch-angle, old branch theater out there—but we have no theaters, no restaurants, no hotels—none of the things that normally bring crowds to downtown areas. We have to depend on our own crowd bringing ideas. So that's why it is important to us to brainstorm the idea of getting crowds constantly.

In the old days, as I say, we limited brainstorming to our Sales Promotion group, but since 1955 brainstorming has taken an important place right across the executive level. Now we brainstorm problems among our sales-promotion group and our operations group.

We have a system in the store that you might be interested in, which you might put into effect quite profitably. We have a luncheon every Friday in our board room, and we alternate between the operations group and the merchandising group.

Now, the operations group is our controller, our advertising manager, our display manager, our building superintendent, our credit manager, our man in charge of all the physicals of the store, as against the building superintendent, who is above him, and one or two more folks who are not in the merchandising end of the business.

Our merchandising group comprises the merchandise managers of all the various divisions, plus the general merchandise manager, the controller again, and the president and myself.

Tiptop executives meet with both groups. One of our most recent uses of brainstorming—and it is so terrific we don't know when we are going to be able to put all of the ideas we got out of it into operation—was a four-day session at a hotel out of town, completely away from the telephone and Buffalo worries, where our Sales Promotion Division for three hours each morning, among other things, brainstormed problems.

The problems we brainstormed were: How can we improve our Mother's day and Father's day Sales Promotions? How can we cut expenses—a real important one this day and time; and one or two other subjects.

We brainstormed these problems before a microphone hooked up with a tape-recording device and brought the tape-recording device back to Buffalo and had the stenographers take off all the ideas—good, bad, indifferent, screwball, wonderful, terrible, it made no difference.

Then, a group of top executives blew away the chaff and picked out what we considered to be the kernels, and then we took these ideas up at a mixed luncheon with the operations group. The operations group was asked to be critical and to bring in that judicial thinking that we kick out of the brainstorming meetings, and see what we had turned up with.

The net result was that we put in two two-hour joint sessions on trying to evaluate the ideas that we came up with out of town, and we have put ten major changes into operation in the store, trying to cut expenses and improve material handling, and a number of other things that before we had just been talking about but had never just beat out to the ultimate in trying to find the solution.

Now, Sattler's has throughout the years brainstormed such things and come up with such ideas as our Bargain Train, where we dramatize the idea that, "Sattler's buys by carloads so you can buy for less."

"Fast Freight to 998." That is our well-known store address in Buffalo.

We say, "From the Eastern Shore to the Wonder Store, from the Golden Gate to 998, the Bargain Train is rattling across the country to bring you the best buys, best because Sattler's buys in carload lots."

We can say that and let it end there, but we brainstormed the problem and said: How can we say it dramatically? We are going into our tenth Bargain Train promotion this fall, and out of brainstorming sessions have come up ideas such as persuading the railroads to line up strings of ten and fifteen decorated freight cars on sidings parallel to heavily traveled streets.

We got out of the brainstorming session the idea of

bringing Mrs. Casey Jones, the widow of old Casey Jones, to Buffalo from Jackson, Tennessee, where the old lady now lives. Her husband was killed, if you remember, fifty-five years ago in Mississippi and became the hero of the most famous and popular folk song ever written.

Mrs. Casey Jones came to Sattler's as a guest, her fare to Buffalo taken care of by the railroad. She was handed over the bridal suite in the Hotel Statler. She appeared on nine separate radio and television shows, each time mentioning the fact that she was here to open Sattler's Bargain Train promotion for that particular year.

We rigged up a whistle to a 100-pound pressure compressed air tank, and the old lady grabbed the lanyard and said, "This here's the way my husband blew his whistle," and there wasn't a dry eye in the crowd, I'll tell you that.

We brainstormed this idea, too: So that she wouldn't go unattended, we had every railroad engineer in the entire area lined up to blow a welcome back to Mrs. Casey Jones, so it sounded like Armistice Day, World War I, if you remember. The Bargain Train was open!

The B & O brought to Buffalo at our request two solid carloads of parade units of a big steam engine, a truck dressed up like a steam locomotive, and another that looked like a diesel locomotive. There were hundreds and hundreds of replicas of famous trains.

We had the Erie bring in a magician for a safety show for the children.

We had the C & O set up in our store a full-sized engine cab, where about fifteen thousand people were able to actually see what a steam locomotive cab looked like. They sat on a seat which had an eccentrically mounted motor underneath that bumped along just as though they were riding along on the tracks, and the kids would see tracks flying by on a screen, and they really had the idea they were in railroad land.

One time when Sattler's had just been the subject of an article in Coronet magazine, which told about some of our screwball brainstormed ideas, a lady from New River, Massachusetts, wrote and said, "I read all about you in Coronet magazine, but I never expect to get to Buffalo. I read about your wonderful bargains. Here is fifty cents. See what you can send me for this."

So we had a brainstorming session on this, and here's what came out of it. We sent an American Airlines Flagship down to Albany, as close as we could get, brought her over to Albany in a cavalcade of automobiles supplied by dealers of that area, brought her back to Buffalo, and ensconced her in the bridal suite of the Hotel Statler, complete with television, which was new there, flowers, and candy.

The next morning she was our guest at the store, where 1,500 employees came down before the store opened and conducted a parade welcoming Mrs. Johnson, and we advertised to the public that we were going to have Mrs. Johnson as our guest and show how hospitable we could be to a customer who had sent fifty cents for a bargain.

We sent her from department to department, with posters saying, "Welcome, Mrs. Johnson. This is your day at 998 Broadway." In each department, where all the doings were reported by a local radio celebrity with a walkie-talkie, going out over the air, she received gifts —rugs, furniture, dresses, coats, suits—to the tune of $1,400 worth of merchandise, all most graciously supplied by our suppliers, who were happy to get into the act. She was wined and dined and taken to all the night clubs and publicized tremendously. Incidentally, Sattler's got a little copy out of this too.

Finally, as she stepped onto the American Airlines airplane to go back to Albany, we handed back to her eleven cents and said, "That only cost you thirty-nine cents at Sattler's. You get a real bargain here."

We also have brainstormed such ideas as our Bargain Airlift: "Sattler's buyers and the nation's flyers bring you the best from all over the world."

Believe it or not, when you go to the people you are going to ask to take part in events like this, surprisingly enough everybody wants to get into the act. When you come up with a screwball idea, people want to be part of it.

We wound up with the Bargain Airlift, which took place at the same time that the Berlin Airlift was at its most dramatic height, and a month or two after the famous Montana haylift was being carried on out west; remember they were dropping bales of hay to starving cattle?

We rode in on a tremendously dramatic idea. We went to the Pentagon with this brainstormed thing which people told us was ridiculous and came back with an all-day show, with three jet teams, two of them from American Aviation groups, one from the Navy, and one from the Air Force.

The Canadian Government heard about our air show, and said, "Can we put in a jet team?" I told them yes, if you will send down thirteen bombers to escort them, and they did.

We had an air show that lasted from nine o'clock in the morning until six o'clock at night. Everybody in Buffalo had a sunburned face that day, May 8, 1949, when we had over $60,000,000 worth of aviation equipment flying for a Buffalo department store!

Superficially that is what it was, but really they were flying for themselves. We went to them with the suggestion that we want to share the impact of our promotional dollar, to help you. Whether you be airline, Air Force, Navy, aviation manufacturer, or whoever you are, if you are interested in promoting the idea of aviation, we want to share our promotional efforts with you.

Well, this idea of casting bread upon the waters really works. You have heard it for thousands of years—we all have—but really, when you try it, it works.

Our brainstormed airlift wound up with such things as every airline in the entire area rerouting its planes to fly over Sattler's. We had floodlights going up into the sky. Three airlines banded together and flew a seven-million-year-old cake of glacier ice from Juneau, Alaska, to cool the cocktails at the press luncheon. That's no lie.

This all-day air show gave the people of Buffalo—the ones who had been going to Curtis, you know, and putting a nut on a bolt all day—a brand-new conception of the importance of American aviation, both civil and military.

It gave the airlines an opportunity to show to the city of Buffalo and to 150,000 people a parade of personal aircraft. It gave the airlines an opportunity to have three thousand people walk through a flying boxcar, where the merchandise was all stowed away. They saw *pianos and furniture and things people never dreamed would be hauled by air.*

We flew lobsters from Maine, strawberries from Florida, tomatoes from Louisiana; we had our buyers up all hours of the night, meeting airplanes at the airport, to take off lots of merchandise and get their pictures taken.

The thing wound up as the National Retail Dry Goods Association's winner of that year for the best co-ordinated campaign, and it began around a table where a bunch of screwballs were brainstorming an idea and tossing out ideas with the knowledge that nobody would criticize them if the ideas were unworkable, stupid, crazy, or what have you.

That gets us down to the very essence of brainstorming, this method of bringing ideas out from behind the woodwork, out of the ratholes, out of the caves of the ocean and the desert and wherever else ideas live that are afraid to come out because some big boss is going to say, "How could you be so stupid?" so the ideas stay there.

We completely wipe out the possibility of anybody's being embarrassed at a brainstorming session and say: Let's have it. We will pick them out. The screwier, the better. We will pick out the good ideas later. But let's have your ideas: good, bad, indifferent, or crazy.

Sattler's has brainstormed itself into what we believe to be the largest store in New York State outside of New York City—some stores have branches now, but we are talking about in one place—and I think that I can honestly say that a tremendous amount of the credit for whatever we have become goes to our techniques of approaching a problem through the brainstorming method.

Notice how Sattler's fitted brainstorming into their operation. They were not afraid to try out things other people said were wacky. They didn't drop hot ideas when they got them; instead, they followed through all the way. With wonderful success.

Retail promotion is just one of the many ways brainstorming can work. BBDO held morning brainstorms for the Republican Party in 1952, a year that was pretty good for the Republican Party.

Brainstorming can help a college in a fund-raising drive, show a city manager how to make a dent in the traffic problem, point the way to increased newspaper circulation.

Bell Aircraft needed a dozen engineers with a very special background. They spent nine thousand dollars on advertising without a single applicant, so they brainstormed how to run an advertisement which would get results. They came up with forty-four ideas. One was to run a job-application form as an advertisement, complete on both sides of a full page in the April 1956 *Aeronautical Engineering Review*. It could be torn out, filled out, and mailed off. They received 114 applications in the first month. When they saw what was happening they tried to yank it out of the next month's issue. It was too late. They received another 264 applications.

Dr. Fred C. Finsterbach of American Cyanamid brainstormed a vital community problem which affects all America in his home town of Berkeley Heights, New Jersey. A much-needed high school was being opposed by a minority who had all sorts of legal power on their side. They thought the cost of the school was too much, and since the community had already exceeded its legal limit of borrowing power, and state authority, as well as local assent, was needed to float a bond issue for the school, the problem was acute. After many regular meetings, Dr. Finsterbach suggested a brainstorm to break through the long discussions of repetitive arguments. In thirty minutes five people came up with twenty-seven ideas of ways to effect a saving in the original cost of the school. Nine were good enough to use, and without any great sacrifice in either the quality of the building, its size, or its educational standards, a savings of $150,000 was made. This cut won immediate approval of the local township committee, which the board needed before going to the state.

Then the board called in the Lay Advisory Committee and the PTA to brainstorm the problem of publicizing the need for the new school. They came up with 108 ideas; thirty-seven were used. Berkeley Heights got its school.

Hospitals have brainstormed the problem of reducing noise; unions have used it to recruit new members. The trick is to apply it to your situation—to your business, your particular problems and personalities. Captain Kangaroo, a fabulously successful television show for children, which was produced almost entirely by a staff under thirty, has a reverse brainstorm after high ratings come out, to think up problems in the program—a good antidote for a swelled head and the deadly attitude of complacency.

You can adapt brainstorming to problems on all levels and all situations. On the same day a company could have brainstorms with different people on problems of production, advertising, personnel, distribution, customer complaints, new product design, packaging, shipping, procurement, administration. The sky's the limit.

In Patterson, New Jersey, Edwin J. MacEwan, executive vice-president and secretary of the Patterson Chamber of Commerce, gave a class for housewives and from it got ideas to help local business concerns.

"What new products in and around the house can you suggest to make work easier and life more pleasant?" he asked.

Answers included frozen breakfasts, electronically operated windows that open and shut by thermostat, foot-controlled water faucets, kitchen chairs that move up and down for children of different sizes, laundry detergents in capsule form.

One even suggested a turntable in the garage so the car wouldn't have to be backed out.

Mrs. Allen Benz took her lessons home. "My husband and I had a chance to go to Europe during the summer," she reports. "But we had a problem. Who would stay with our two children? I tried brainstorming and came up with a solution I never would have thought of before—hiring a schoolteacher as a full-time baby sitter."

The New Brunswick, New Jersey, Presbyterian Church has used brainstorming in its planning conferences. Here are some of their results:

FELLOWSHIP

1 *Members should not sit in the same seat Sunday after Sunday, that they may get acquainted with more people.*

2 *"Know your names" month. Have names printed on cards and mailed out to congregation, and have them worn when attending church. Printing to be good size.*

3 *Pictures of new members to be taken and placed somewhere with their names attached, that others may get ac-*

quainted with the name and familiar with the person. Perhaps these pictures could appear in the church calendar.

4 *At dinner meetings, get acquainted with the person to the left of you and to the right and also across from you.*

5 *Each time you come to church, try to get acquainted with someone else.*

6 *Say "Good morning" to each one you meet and you will soon find out who are members and who are visitors.*

7 *Have some slogan for the month such as "Would you help me with your name?"*

8 *Have a complete Church Roll, including a picture of each member.*

9 *Organize a Couples' Club.*

MUSIC

1 *Get those who like to sing together and perhaps organize a Glee Club.*

2 *Give the choir a rest and have Glee Club in the choir loft a couple times a year.*

3 *Have "spotters" to pick out those with good voices and give names to choir.*

4 *Ushers should try to group people together. When you hear people singing around you, it makes you want to sing —thus bettering congregational singing.*

5 *A recognition dinner for choir members is being planned for May.*

6 *Planning for a choir of sixty voices. This will encourage singing in the congregation.*

7 *Sing old hymns of the church.*

8 *Place choir in the congregation sometime.*

9 *Have special musical services, such as Christmas Carol Sing.*

10 *Members should send in suggestions to Music Committee. Response is now being sung preceding prayer rather than following prayer, to inspire more prayerful attitude. A prelude quietly played places people in a more worshipful attitude. (Sometimes noise is so great, organ cannot be heard.) Should the organist play a postlude, or should people be dismissed in a prayerful attitude?*

11 *Change hour of Bible classes in order to hear children sing.*

12 *People remain seated at close of service.*

13 *Hear all three choirs at church service.*

MEMBERSHIP

1 *Be sure that there are no questions in the minds of new people. Everything should be explained to them.*

2 *Try a "Big Brother or Big Sister" movement for a period of six weeks.*

3 *Have new members assigned to specific people. (This has been done.)*

4 *Introduce people to special activities. This can be done by individuals telling new members about certain activities in the church in which they may be interested.*

5 *Put new members on committees as soon as they unite with the church.*

6 *Have commission and committee members attend New Members classes in order that they may get acquainted with the new members and familiarize the new people with the various activities in the church.*

7 *Is there enough follow-up on new members to see that they become active?*

8 *Train new people by using them as co-workers.*

Trans World Airlines recently held a brainstorm session in Paris on how to improve passenger service. Here are a few of the 110 ideas turned out in thirty minutes. Notice how often you laughingly read a list like this and then pause to say, "Hey, that isn't a bad idea after all!"

Make available "Do Not Disturb" buttons or clothespin signs for passengers to wear in flight so the stewardess does not wake them up.

Have a small projector to show movies in flight.

Individual loud-speakers in seats so people can tune in on music.

Better advice to passengers when flights have been delayed or canceled.

Put families with children in same part of plane.

Have certain amount of seats facing each other for people who wish to play cards or know each other.

Have pills for passengers to alleviate fear.

(Hitchhike! Serve martinis instead of pills.)

Serve milk to everybody.

Have escalator gangplanks.

Have mystery books in pocket seats.

Hold air pools on landing times as they do with ship pools.

Hold Bingo games.

Hold collective games.

Have safer drivers on buses to the airport.

Make Gander Airport more attractive.

Take average weight of passengers and if under this, passenger is entitled to more luggage weight.

Make a study of why people are afraid in the air.

Have small dance band and dancing on board.

(Hitchhike! Have instruments on board for passengers who wish to join in the band.)
Have toys for dogs on airplanes.
Banish all dogs from airplanes.
(Hitchhike! Banish all animals from airplanes.)
Establish special flights for animal lovers.
Give out passenger lists to passengers.
Introduce passengers to each other on the flight.
Re-establish all-first-class Ambassador Flights.
Give out recipes that can be made with air (soufflés).
Good-behavior medal for children who behave on flight.
Dishonorable discharges for those who don't.
Take pictures of passengers in transit and forward to their home-town newspapers.
Take polls on airplanes on how to improve TWA *service.*
Increase difference in comfort between tourist and first-class passengers.
Eliminate sleeper socks.
Establish ways to appease passengers who can't get seats during the rush season.

You may think you have a unique problem—and, in fact, you may. But don't dismiss brainstorming as a way to beat it. Try it on for size, and you'll be amazed how well it will fit.

TROUBLES ARE A BRAINSTORMER'S BEST FRIEND

*how you can turn
your problems
into advantages*

profits from frustration

*turning temper
into cash*

the nose for needs

*a company
which thrives
on problems*

*how you can
find problems*

*case histories
of companies
which turned problems
into profits*

*how you
can do
the same*

Troubles are a brainstormer's best friend. This apparent paradox is true because problems are the raw materials which brainstorming turns into valuable ideas.

Brainstorming is a device which does not best dance the minuet of polite discussion or wander vaguely among the gardens of philosophical thought. It is a shirt-sleeved laborer who rolls up his sleeves and goes to work to solve specific problems with specific solutions.

You will find that it eats up problems at a frightful rate. It is like the new electronic computers which solve the most involved bookkeeping or calculating problems in hours. Its owners have to hunt up new jobs for the monster's appetite. The same thing can be true of brainstorming if you really put it to work at every level and in every department of your business.

This is an extremely healthy situation in which to find yourself, for problem-finding is the cornerstone of creative thinking. The businessman who sees no problems but sits back, smugly content with his methods, is the businessman who goes bankrupt. The businessman who continues to see the same old problems and accept them as an unchanging part of his life is just as limited and just as doomed.

Problems—seemingly insoluble, irritating, frustrating, aggravating, frightening problems—are the birthplace of new ideas. Duncan Hines was a printing salesman who had a hard time finding decent places to eat while he was traveling his territory. You all know what he did with that problem. He sent out Christmas cards to his friends who were on the road, recommending good places to eat. The demand for them became so great that recommending good food for many travelers became his career—and a very profitable one it is.

In 1948 a New York high school teacher received a letter from a California educator who had a problem: he needed a good but inexpensive New York hotel where he could live for the summer. The teacher had a problem: he wanted to go to California for the summer, but he had little money. Solution: they swapped homes and later founded Vacations Residence Exchange, which provides a center for hundreds of people who solve their vacation problem by swapping homes.

Seven years ago William Schwann lost his temper trying to keep track of the new spate of long-playing records. He carried his anger a step farther than most of us. He organized the highly successful Schwann Long-Playing Record Catalogue, which is standard in the field today.

J. D. Dole realized in 1932 that he had a major problem. He had more pineapples growing than he could sell in conventional ways. He had to find new ways to sell pineapple and create a market for his new ways. He made pineapple juice and got people to drink it.

President Fargo of the American Express Company took a European trip in 1891 and became furious at the time it took to have his letter of credit cleared at every stop. The result: Travelers Cheques. Mrs. Louise Bubser Gray was desperately sick in the 1880's. Her husband had to plead for long moments with a factory executive to use the only phone in the area to call a doctor. Between 1888 and 1902 he was granted twenty-three basic patents on the pay telephone.

Listen to Don G. Mitchell, now chairman and president of the very successful electronics company, Sylvania Electric Products Inc., tell you what happened when he was faced with that age-old problem—the huge, successful competitor in another job.

Too many smaller companies develop an inferiority complex about their big competitors and hide their lights under a bushel basket. They seem to forget that the little fellow can frequently outmaneuver the big one, and this is what I mean: After cutting my teeth on the retail goods business for several years, I joined a soft-drink company in 1939 with the idea of cutting a few chunks off the market of our biggest competitor. I knew absolutely nothing about the soft-drink business. Everything I knew I had picked up as a consumer. So I read everything I could about peddling soft drinks and, lo and behold, I came to the conclusion that the big competitor was more than a little vulnerable. They had left a hole a mile wide in their distribution. They had concentrated so much on selling their product over the soda fountain and for consumption on the premises that they had forgotten that sometimes, once in a while, the consumer might want to drink one in his home.

So we pulled a switch. We concentrated on the tremendous home market and forgot about the fountain business and the on-the-premises stuff. We brought out a six-bottle container and promoted the home market with all sorts of tricks and strong point-of-sale promotion. Our market curve soared right off the chart.

In 1853 James E. Liddy of Watertown, New York, had a wonderful ride on a buggy which had coil-spring cushions. That was no problem—but sleeping at home in his hard bed was. He developed coil springs to replace the rope used in beds at the time. He saw his real problem and solved it.

Fred Barton, an actor, had a hard time learning his lines during the necessarily short rehearsals when he first appeared in TV. His answer was the Teleprompter, which is standard in the industry today.

An insurance salesman by the name of Waterman had a hard time getting customers to sign contracts with his blotty, leaky pen. He took his pen apart and devised the Waterman pen. In 1927 a twenty-nine-year-old father blew his top at the infuriating job of mashing cooked peas through a kitchen strainer with a spoon. It took him hours. His name was Dan Gerber.

All of these trouble finders had one thing in common. I call it a nose for needs. They spotted a problem, and in solving that problem saw that others had a need for the same solution.

Let the Johnson & Johnson Company tell a story about a nose for needs:

> It was a great joke in the Order Department of Johnson & Johnson. Five thousand rolls of surgical tape ordered by a druggist in Detroit who couldn't sell that much tape to all the hospitals in the city.
>
> He had probably added an extra zero by mistake, suggested someone. Send him 500 rolls. Back came an indignant telephone call from the druggist. He had or-

dered 5000 rolls. Why only 500? He needed the rest of the shipment and fast.

The Sales Department lost no time in sending their Detroit representative to determine the reason for such an order. The salesman's report was brief and to the point. An auto-body manufacturer was buying the surgical tape at the rate of 200 rolls a week—he had found a practical answer to masking two-tone paint jobs. That was the beginning of Permacel Tape Corporation.

From this one clue, Johnson & Johnson realized the great possibilities for pressure-sensitive tapes in industry. The problem of exploration and development was turned over to one of the Johnson & Johnson subsidiaries, the Revolite Company, who were then making waterproof sheeting.

Research indicated that there were a great many ways for pressure-sensitive tape to serve industry—to improve products—to cut down costs and speed production. The indicated potential justified the formation of the Industrial Tape Corporation, a wholly owned subsidiary. Production started in 1937 and PERMACEL *and* TEXCEL *were introduced to the market.*

During the first three years, it was necessary to add more and more space, and increase facilities to meet a growing demand. In June, 1940, plans were approved for one of the most modern industrial plants in the United States.

Anticipating continued growth, these plans provided for an 80 per cent increase in future production. In March of 1941, the new plant was opened, but the demand for PERMACEL *and* TEXCEL *was so great that it already far exceeded the entire maximum capacity of the plant, including the 80 per cent planned expansion. New additions to the plant were started immediately. Since then this plant has more than tripled in size.*

The thousands of uses for pressure-sensitive tapes under so many varied conditions call for highly technical and scientific research. These laboratory tests are constantly improving quality, solving new problems, producing tapes exactly suited to particular needs. As plant facilities expanded and new uses for tape developed, it was necessary to substantially expand the Research Department.

By 1952 when the ultramodern laboratories of Johnson & Johnson were completed, a whole new wing was set aside for PERMACEL *and* TEXCEL *research exclusively. The acceptance of* PERMACEL *has made it advisable to change the name of the company to* PERMACEL *Tape Corporation. Its main plant covers fifteen acres, and today this company is a leader in the manufacture of pressure-sensitive tapes—an industry that has grown from an idea to a volume of more than three hundred million dollars a year.*

They had a nose for needs.

The Polaroid Company, manufacturers of the fabulously successful Land camera, which takes a picture and produces the finished product in a minute, is a prime example of a company which has grown by its nose for needs.

They've pushed their camera as a novelty at conventions, a must at family gatherings, showing how a Polaroid camera can be used at charity benefits, church gatherings, fairs, carnivals, fund-raising booths.

They proved that this camera can be used to advantage to

record instrument readings during test flights at the United Airlines maintenance base, and by an antique dealer in New York who uses the Land camera when he locates pieces for interior decorators in other cities. In a minute he has pictures of the piece in the mail on the way to the prospective buyer. The company has also plugged its use in increasing advertising art production; speeding loans by getting quick shots of property; helping contractors support bids, show material damaged on arrival, support insurance claims, and illustrate progress reports. The company has proved its value in preserving pictures of plant processes or problems for later study.

Every time they have an idea they push it in the appropriate industry. Now the Land camera is used to back up field reports of adjusters, in shops to develop safety techniques and equipment, by police to get quick shots of kidnaping victims, accidents, finger- and footprints. Polaroid has even tested its value in making photo patterns for shop production. Other companies have used it for identification of material in warehousing areas—when something is stored away, a shot is taken of its location and clipped to the inventory record. One company which sells tires even uses the camera to take pictures of bad tires on cars and send them to the auto owners with a strong sales pitch.

It is common logic that before you can solve any problem you first have to spot the problem. Yet this is not as easy as it seems, for there is a natural tendency in every human being to hide problems, or better yet, just stick his head in the sand and ignore them.

Things are starting to back up in the shipping room. Is the

foreman going to come to his boss and say, "I'm having some trouble, and I don't know just where it is."

Usually not.

If he did come to his boss, and if the boss was the right kind of executive, they might sit down and root out the problem. Brainstorming can often reveal these problems, and once you have discovered a problem you are halfway to a solution, for there is a great creative skill in spotting the right problem.

One production genius I know refuses to hold meetings in his front office. When there is a problem he insists on going out to the shop, to the very spot where a machine is broken down or a log jam of parts has piled up. "Often I see an entirely different problem than the one they tell me about," he explains.

How do you find problems?

One way is to sit back and dream up an ideal operation. Set a sky-high ideal for your business with procurement, production, and sales rolling along perfectly. Then match up current operations—which you have come to accept as normal—and you'll find plenty of problems.

Another twist on the same thing is to set a goal in a certain department. For example, set a sales goal in your territory of twice what you sell today. Then dig into the reasons you are not meeting it. Thinking why you can't possibly hit that goal, you may say, "We don't sell to the supermarkets." Whoa, there. "Why don't we sell to supermarkets?" Then, "How can I sell my product to the supermarkets?" You've got a problem, brother, and a brainstormed solution can increase your sales 100 per cent.

Be a good listener. A great many executives never hear of problems because they won't listen. First, build up an atmosphere in which employees will come to you. Don't have your subordinates growling, "He won't listen if you tell him anyway." That's a common complaint. Next, is this one: "If you do tell him he doesn't hear."

Too many of us are discourteous and inefficient listeners. We assume a thoughtful expression and let our minds wander over our golf score, or what we'll say at the next meeting of our luncheon club. We fumble with our pencil and doodle; we mentally doubt what the speaker is saying, or leap ahead to answer and argue with his conclusions; we discount his words on past prejudices.

The good interrogator, the policeman or the attorney, always listens to every word, ready to pick up any bit of information which is dropped or even hinted at in the conversation.

Make it a habit to listen to people. You'll be surprised at what you'll learn.

Your eyes are still the best problem hunter you've got, however. Make it a practice to walk through your plant, visit your customers, not just call them on the phone. See your market, your product. Look at your product in the factory and on the shelves. Watch the people around you. Keep looking.

Let the Reynolds Metals Company tell you about what happened when a vice-president saw a minor problem around the shop and kept his eyes as well as his mind open:

THE SCENE: *Louisville, Kentucky.* THE TIME: *September, 1951.* OCCASION: *Remodeling of the Reynolds building.*

CHAPTER THIRTEEN

PRINCIPALS: *A carpenter and Clarence F. Manning, the Reynolds vice-president who heads the firm's sales development division.*

Entering the building that September morning, Manning spied the carpenter cutting aluminum trim molding with an ordinary wood-working crosscut saw. A hacksaw, normally used for cutting metal, lay nearby. "Son," said Manning, who has been in the metal business with Reynolds for thirty years, "you're going to have a saw with no teeth in it if you keep that up. Why don't you use that hacksaw? You can't cut metal with wood tools."

The carpenter, with due respect for vice-presidential rank but with the assurance of a man who knows whereof he speaks, replied: "You may be right, Mr. Manning, but I don't think so. I've been cutting aluminum with this saw for months, and I can't find any damage. Maybe you can."

Manning inspected the saw, and indeed, it seemed to be in excellent shape. He took a length of the metal to his office. Other company officials inquired about the ordinary-looking length of aluminum on his desk. "That," said Manning, "happens to be some of our aluminum they're using in the remodeling work downstairs. Guy this morning was cutting it with a crosscut saw. Said he had been for weeks. Didn't hurt the saw a bit. Think we might have a good item here for the man with a home workshop."

"Manning," they told him, "you've been a good vice-president. We like you. We'd like to have you stay around. But your idea won't work—you've got to have special tools to cut metal!"

Vice-president Manning was unimpressed. He asked

for, and received, a special appropriation to set up a complete home workshop in that same building. He hired a cabinet maker named Bill Miller, who had virtually no experience in working with metal.

"Bill," he told the new man, "go out and buy tools and set up a home workshop. Get ordinary tools—hand tools and power tools. Buy 'em at places you'd buy them if this was to be your own workshop. Don't get any special high-priced tools. Set up a workshop, and when you've done it, report back to me."

In a couple of weeks, the workshop was ready. Miller was waiting in Manning's office one Monday morning.

"Mr. Manning, I've got a workshop. I bought all those tools. What do you want me to do with them?"

"Bill," was the reply, "here's a supply of aluminum. I want you to take it to your workshop. Use it on your power tools. Work it with your hand tools. Make things with it. I want to see what you can do."

Miller's face clouded. This man, he thought, may be a vice-president, but I'm going to keep him out of my workshop. "Mr. Manning," he declared, "you can't use those tools on metal. It'll ruin 'em. I've got a jointer-planer down there, and a lot of other good tools I paid good money for. Do you want me to break them up the first day?"

"Try it, Bill," was the reply. "If you're right, we ruin some tools. If I'm right, we've got a new product."

What Miller didn't know was that Manning, working with metallurgists, had selected an aluminum alloy and temper strong enough for workshop use, yet softer than tool steel. The softer metal, he reasoned, wouldn't damage tools any more than wood materials.

Manning was right. The aluminum worked beautifully. Even the sensitive jointer-planer was undamaged after repeated use with the metal. Power saws, drills . . . all the hand and power tools . . . were tried, and none were dulled any more than they would be by wood materials.

That was the beginning of the new home workshop material now being marketed nationwide by Reynolds Metals—it's called Do-It-Yourself Aluminum. The metal, especially engineered for home workshop use, comes in a variety of shapes and sizes, including sheet, rod, bar, tubing, angle. Even roll-formed and extruded sections designed especially for home-built windows and screens are available in hardware stores and building-supply outlets.

Reynolds furnishes a free instruction book for use of the material at retail outlets where it is sold. Plans for simple, yet useful, items for the home and farm are included. The usefulness of the material is based on the fact that it ". . . may be worked with hand or power tools with no more dulling than would result from materials in the wood category. . . ."

Another way to find problems is to read. That doesn't mean just the Podunk journal. Read the Sunday New York *Times*, *Time Magazine*, the *Saturday Evening Post*, the *Reader's Digest*, your trade journals. Read business books and technical books. Many companies subscribe to clipping services which keep them reading material from all over the country in a variety of fields. Surveys have shown that the higher executives rise, the more they read. They are looking for problems and for ideas.

For example, the president of the Lucky Tiger Manufacturing Company of Kansas City saw a new problem when he was reading. The result was a new product with a barrel of profits. Here's the way that company tells the story:

> *Stephen W. Harris read a brief United Press item, datelined Port Huron, Mich., that barbers reported the first run in decades on sales of mustache wax. Reason for the sudden popularity of mustache wax, the news item said, was that "teen-agers have found the wax perfect to make a crew-cut haircut stand up straight."*
>
> *Reading the item, it occurred to Harris that the style might not just be a momentary fad. The trend to shorter cuts fits into the patterns of outdoor and casual styles that were becoming an accepted part of suburban life throughout the country. Crew cuts had become of age, as it were, and presented a wonderful market for a wax especially adapted to the proper cutting and dressing of short haircuts.*
>
> *After much experimentation, Harris evolved a pomade with a petrolatum-type base to which had been added long fiber waxes, giving it the proper consistency to make hair stand up to a proper crew cut. He christened it "Butch" Hair Wax Dressing.*
>
> *Test-marketed in Kansas City with the Katz Drug Chain in a unique type of co-operative TV program, the new hair wax dressing was an immediate success. The pent-up demand for mustache wax was transferred to the new product. Promotion was expanded to thirty-one TV areas and sales movement reached nine dozen jars a week in one store, the highest reported movement of any one men's hair preparation product.*

The man who wants to have ideas that make a difference should not stop trying to be creative when he leaves the brainstorm session. He should make the process of having brainstorms an integral part of his life. He should be consciously seeking problems, seeing new things and new combinations of things that will keep stimulating his subconscious.

One of the best ways to solve problems is to stop them when they are small enough to solve easily. The president of one company holds regular sessions he calls "Clouds on the Horizon Meeting." The group is asked to bring up any areas in which problems may occur. "We try to smoke out little troubles that have not yet developed into real problems," he explains.

Perhaps a vice-president in charge of the future—a sort of pre-trouble shooter—could do the same job. It's an important one. And once he has spotted the problems, he can brainstorm them.

The Downingtown Paper Company of Downingtown, Pennsylvania, even added a new suggestion system in which employees were asked to submit entries to find the Problem of the Month and receive a twenty-five-dollar gift.

One man who has put his problems to work is Lewis H. Glaser, president of Revell Inc., one of the nation's top plastic toy producers today. One evening in 1949 he was listening to Jack Benny's radio program, when he heard him say, "Rochester, get out the Maxwell, and we'll drive to Palm Springs."

Something clicked in Glaser's mind. He had a tiny plastics business, but he got a large idea. Why not make a plastic miniature of Jack Benny's Maxwell? His plant was in the doldrums, and they needed new products. He went to work, and at the annual toy fair in New York he filled orders for a quarter of a million of them.

Awhile ago he was fiddling with one of those models while he paced a hospital waiting-room, waiting for the birth of his first child. Like all fathers, his hand was none too steady. He dropped the toy and it broke. He had a problem. How to put it together?

Wait. What if plastic toys—ship models, plane models, models of tanks, guns, western vehicles, knights in shiny armor—were made of plastic parts which the customer could put together himself? He worked out the plans right in the waiting-room. Since then, Revell has sold sixty-five million hobby kits and sparked an entire new hobby industry.

The right question—Glaser's, how can you put them together—is often half the distance to the right answer. For example, Rand Development Company in Cleveland was asked by a metal-working company how to dispose economically of a highly acid steel-cleaning liquid. Rand saw a different question. Is the cleaning fluid needed? It wasn't. They designed a mechanical method of cleaning the steel which was more efficient and far more economical.

Another time Rand was asked to design a switch that wouldn't burn out, to do the job done by the twenty-dollar ones the company was replacing every few days. Rand engineers saw that the motors were the wrong type for the switches. Conversion cost little, so they changed the motors and installed a one-dollar switch. Problem solved.

Here's the result of a brainstorm I held which should help us all. It was on the subject of HOW TO DEVELOP A NOSE FOR NEEDS:

Watch for ideas in normal reading.

Listen *to others.*

Build idea file.

Try to reduce problems to records of some sort so that you know where to concentrate with ideas.

Make use of those around you in assembling ideas.

Be alert to irritations.

Hunt for trouble spots.

Keep an open mind—don't be restricted by tradition.

Remember nothing is perfect.

Take time to be inquisitive.

Learn to ask questions.

Reward people for what might result from flushing out an idea.

Use an "idea trap" to record ideas when they occur.

Develop a sensitivity or more acute awareness of other potential uses of something.

Read material on what others have done by developing new ideas.

Read as much current news as possible.

Try to visualize what is needed in any material or process to make it fit your need exactly rather than almost.

Read hobby books and those that illustrate imaginative developments of others.

Stop, look, and listen.

Talk to people in fields outside your usual circle.

When you are irritated by something, improve it creatively.

Read widely.

By maintaining a universal interest in anything and everything.

By keeping your mind open at all times—hence, always observing everything—everywhere.

Executives I have talked with around the country have made a number of suggestions about how to develop a nose for needs, and I would like to pass some of them along to you. Most of them suggest that you first practice with small problems and then build up to larger problems. Then they advise that you should read a great deal and always watch for ideas during your reading. The same thing is true during your TV viewing and your radio listening. And every time you get an idea it should be jotted down and filed away.

The man who wants a nose for needs must be a good listener. Few people pay attention to what other people say. The man who is looking for ideas must listen carefully and intelligently and be perfectly willing to sacrifice his own comments for someone else's. He should keep an open mind; look for trouble spots and listen to the irritations and complaints of others. You have to find problems before you can find solutions.

Most idea men purposely associate with people who are mentally stimulating to them, seeking out acquaintances who come from different backgrounds, or who are in different professions. The man who wants to be an effective idea producer must maintain his enthusiasm and his curiosity at all times. He should not be afraid to be nosy, to ask questions, to look below the surface, and as he finds out more about the world around him, he will find it is a lot more fun to live in it as well.

THE COMPLEAT BRAINSTORMER

*how to look at
your world creatively*

*how you can
invite brainstorms*

*ways you can
solve your problems
creatively*

*how you can make
a check list*

*how you can make
an idea bank and
an idea museum*

your own idea trap

Brainstorming teaches us the importance of spontaneous, un-inhibited thought. It makes us realize that even when we look at old, familiar problems we can see new solutions if we don't let preconceived judgment and prejudice rule our mind. It shows us how new and important ideas come to those who aren't obsessed with what can't be done.

One scientist, in talking about a genius who has had little formal training, told me, "He doesn't have a great deal to un-learn. Most of us with Ph.D. degrees know all the things that can't be done. He doesn't. He tries them, and they work."

A city editor told a writing friend of mine, "A good reporter is forever astounded at the obvious."

This is important. We must, the older we grow, the more experienced we become, cultivate a naïveté about our work. The fact that this is difficult explains why most scientific dis-coveries are made by young men. They don't know what can't be done.

I don't mean that we should throw away our professional training and years of experience and try to be dewy-eyed youngsters with gray hair and bulging waistlines. The mid-dle-aged adolescent is no help to any business. I do mean that there is a place for judgment—and it is in the working out of an idea, not in the process of having it.

We should all encourage in ourselves the insight of the little boy who came along when a huge trailer truck was stuck under a low bridge. Truck drivers, state police, highway officials, engineers were talking about jacking up the bridge, cutting the truck's top off with a blow torch, when the lad piped up, "Why not let the air out of the tires?"

We must try to do the same thing. We must look at problems simply and clearly. Tied in with this is the need for a sense of wonder about our world, a curiosity and a willingness to keep looking at things in new ways.

When we look at a problem without an apparent solution we should approach it from all sides, mentally at least; turn it inside out, upside down. Add to it, subtract from it, divide, multiply, break it down into its components, look for similar problems and solutions—and opposite ones,

This ability to look at things, the common, ordinary things that we are in constant contact with, in a new light is a skill which we must apply to all our lives.

If you are trying to improve a toy, you should not only look at it as a toy manufacturer, but as the buyer of a toy department and as his salesclerk. You must also resee it from the point of view of your own production man, and then you must try to look at it from the point of view of the youngster for whom it is intended. You should also look at it as a parent, and as a grandparent (surely the world's biggest buyers of toys). You must examine the toy for its color and know which colors children like. Since children use their hands much more than adults, you should think of its texture; you must consider its durability and its safety and its simplicity and its profit.

If we do, we will be far more productive brainstormers. We will contribute more ideas in brainstorm sessions—but more than that, we will find ourselves having brainstorms as we walk along the street, wait to call on a customer, cut the lawn, fish, stop for a red light, read the paper, shower, sit in conference, repair a leaky faucet.

We can and should kill the old pro in all of us, the gnarled old grump who growls, "We did that twenty years ago," whenever a new idea is mentioned.

There are ways we can keep our minds constantly awake to new ideas and possibilities. In this chapter I shall present some of them, for the brainstorming attitude should be a way of life, an important part of all our waking and sleeping hours.

One way to get new ideas is to use a check list. There are all sorts of such lists. For example, the Department of Commerce puts out one: "100 Questions for Prospective Manufacturers." Many industry associations and publications publish check lists, which can force us to think of all sorts of details and approaches we may have missed.

The General Electric Company, which has had a creative thinking course for almost twenty years, puts out a fat book of *Physical Laws and Effects*. On its title page is this simple statement: "An engineer who utilizes only the commonly known physical laws and effects tends to limit himself to conventional engineering practices. This compilation contains many uncommon phenomena which may be valuable in the solution of your problems."

The book is indexed so that physicists may, for example, look up mechanical, electronic, chemical laws in solving a problem in another scientific area.

John E. Arnold, professor in charge of the Creative Engineering Laboratory at M.I.T., sent out a "Check List Solitaire" for Christmas, based on Alex Osborn's ideas. It became so popular, he has published it in book form, small enough to be carried in the pocket and referred to when you are actually facing a problem.

Make up your own list from Chapter Five (Pages 99–101). Paste it on the bottom of a desk drawer, carry it in a notebook or your head, but use it.

Look around you, and you will see how other people have thought up, if not new ideas at least new and profitable variations by the use of such a list.

One important thing a list does is to remind you of the importance of structures. Each time you see a structure pattern, you see a whole variety of sequential ideas. *Reader's Digest* leads to *Science Digest* and a whole line of digest magazines. Pocket Books to Penguin Books to Anchor Books; transistors in guided missiles to transistors in car radios; Book-of-the-month to Fruit-of-the-month to Gift-of-the-month to Candy-of-the-month to History Book Club to Civil War Book Club, and so on.

You'll be surprised how often a simple mental trick like reversing a problem can often solve it. Charles F. Kettering, General Motors' genius, has a dramatic example of how reversing a problem can solve it. Here it is in his own words:

> *So our industry has grown up on the principle of letting the job be the boss, and I still think that is a good thing to do, because you can't expect material to do something just because you think it should.*
>
> *We have had a lot of jobs like that. Take the extreme pressure lubricants. Lubricating oils are very old, and some time ago at Cornell University there was developed a lubricating testing machine based on a railroad jour-*

nal. Many tests had been run, a lot of tables plotted out, and six thousand pounds per square inch of projected area of the bearing was the highest that they could go with the best lubricating oils then available. We had built a small testing machine at our laboratories and our figures checked very well with this.

Now what more could you ask?

So I said, "Well, let's just try an experiment. Let's suppose that the lubricating oil testing machine is a dangerous weapon. It belongs to your worst enemy, and he can kill you and your family with it. But you can pick the lubricant for it. What would you recommend if you were picking the poorest thing in the world to lubricate it with? What would you specify?"

We all thought about it and finally picked a material called monochlormethane ether, which is practically the same as is used to put you to sleep when you are going to have a surgical operation. It is so thin it has no viscosity at all. You can pour it on your hand and blow on it and it is all gone. You couldn't pour it in a warm machine as a liquid, it would evaporate at once, so we took the cap off the ether can, soldered a tube on it, ran the tube over to the bearing machine and sealed it into the oil hole. Then we put a warm towel around the can and the vapors went through the tube to the bearing. Since there was no liquid in the bearing, it must run absolutely dry.

We had made bets on how long it would last—how much pressure it would take. One man had nerve enough to guess 150 pounds. That was the highest. We started to load up the machine very gently and carefully, and to make a long story short, we ran out of weights at thirty thousand pounds. Everybody was amazed; they said, "It can't be." But we tried it over and over again, and we got some more weights. I think it stuck up around thirty-six thousand pounds—five or six times the load of the best oil.

We brought the oil engineers in and showed it to them. They said, "The only thing that makes us sore is that we didn't do it. This is our business, not yours."

"But," I said, "you couldn't have done it. You have graded oils for so long on their viscosity that you would have fired anybody who proposed using something like this, that didn't have any viscosity feel to it."

Well, that was the beginning of the so-called extreme pressure lubrication which came just about the time we were developing the hypoid gears, and you couldn't have run hypoid gears if it hadn't been for these lubricants. There are many things that you couldn't do today if it wasn't for these lubricants.

Now what did we do? All that had been done in lubricating oils before that was to test the affinity of one molecule of oil for another. This is called viscosity. When you put pressure on them, you found that you pushed them apart and you had no lubrication. But the oils with no viscosity at all formed a chemical bond more like the nap on plush, and this took much more pressure to break through than did the viscosity film. It completely changed the concept of what you could do with lubricating oils.

Here's a case where a fellow had a chain reaction that hooked a couple of ideas together and built a better mousetrap:

William Henricks and his wife were visiting friends who

had set a conventional spring-type mousetrap in their kitchen earlier in the evening. While they were playing cards, the trap was sprung and a mouse caught. To Mr. Henricks this was an ordinary event. To his hosts, it was a catastrophe. The wife ran to her bedroom, screaming. The husband ran to a closet and got a broom, then went to the kitchen, opened the outside door and swept the mouse and the trap out without ever touching it. It reminded their guests of the comics seen so often of a woman standing screaming on a chair with a little mouse looking up at her.

Later, when Mr. and Mrs. Henricks were at home, Mrs. Henricks showed her husband a dozen polyethylene tumblers that she had purchased that day. The combination of the mouse incident and the tumblers planted the "seed thought" for the "Sanitrap," a transparent plastic tube with poison inside. The mouse crawls in, eats the poison, and the whole trap is tossed away without anyone touching the mouse.

The same thought process occurred when someone saw a couple of crossed knives and made a pair of scissors. Then the pair of scissors gave someone the idea for a pair of pliers.

Another way to get new ideas is to turn the problem upside down, inside out, or backward. Henry Ford didn't worry about how to get workmen to the parts needed in an automobile, but how to get the parts to them. That was the basic idea of the assembly line.

The clock-radio came about when someone thought of combining two bedroom facilities—then someone else came along and thought about dividing it. New clock radios are marketed which can be separated so the clock timer can be used in the kitchen, while the radio is playing out on the patio.

You can borrow or adapt, ring in the changes on a good idea. Make it larger or smaller, thinner or thicker, lighter or heavier. To make sure he tries all combinations, the effective creative thinker uses a check list the same way an airline pilot does before he takes off. He will develop a check list on the subjects in the area in which he has problems he has to solve oftenest. For example, he might have a plastic-enclosed list hung behind his desk or over his workbench: "300 ways to package plants," "250 promotional ideas," "176 ways to reach customers," or "476 ways to fasten wood."

You can use the classified section of your phone book as a check list or an inspiration list. You might even go to your library and look through the yellow pages from other cities. The Sears Roebuck catalogue can be an inspiration stimulant, and I know the Montgomery Ward catalogue used to be known as a "wish book." Charles Whiting of McCann-Erickson has a Forced Relationship Technique which does this. You apply the attributes of an object to suggest changes in another object.

For example, if you are manufacturing power boats, you might well take the time to examine what the car manufacturers have found about the desires of people. What do they like in car interiors, what designs, what colors, what textures, what kind of windows, what gadgets? You should examine the new personal airplanes as well as the airliners. You might visit the latest ocean liners and even the small and very popular suburban homes. The important attributes of the interiors of cars, planes, ships, homes will suggest salable changes you can make in the interior design of your boats.

A good brainstormer never takes the obvious for granted. He knows the best ideas seem obvious after they have been developed. Take an ordinary envelope. Look at it to see the changes that creative thinking has made.

> *Why lick the stamps? The embossed stamped envelope.*
> *Why type return address? It's printed on.*
> *Why type the address on the letter and the envelope as well? The window envelope.*
> *There is color coding for air mail.*
> *Then someone tore the envelope apart and found out how much wasted writing area there was inside. He invented the air letter, which became World War II's V-mail.*
> *Someone else lost a slip of paper in an inter-office envelope, so it is made with holes in it.*

There are a hundred variations. Large envelopes, small envelopes, Kraft paper envelopes, and onion-skin envelopes. There are even envelopes which have a smaller envelope on the outside—that way your letter goes first-class, and the material in the big envelope third or fourth class. There is a self-sealing envelope flavored with peppermint to satisfy the most sensitive tongue puckerer.

Challenge any assumptions. There is nothing sacred about the envelope, the umbrella, or the automobile as we know it. Sylvania has made a wonderful product by saying, "Why should lamp bulbs be white?" and marketing colored ones.

Finding the right frame of reference and breaking out of the wrong one is a valuable step in creative thinking. For example, when the Pennsylvania Railroad had a problem getting their switching engines around their yards, they naturally thought up all sorts of switching engines—that ran on tracks. The problem was solved when someone broke out of that frame of reference and developed a switching engine which runs on great rubber wheels and can be run along tracks or, just as easily, across them.

Again and again it's productive to look for new uses for old devices. The New York Telephone Company today makes four million dollars a year from correct time and weather forecast calls. New products, on the other hand, fail or succeed on new uses; the helicopter, for instance. If it hadn't been tried in rescues, for traffic checks, on low-level photography, repairing remote high-tension wires, it wouldn't be the basis of a growing industry today. The phone company needs new uses for old devices; the helicopter industry, old uses for a new device. When we discovered radioactive isotopes we had to find how to use them. We have solutions seeking problems as well as problems seeking solutions.

Make a list of all possible uses of a product or a method. For example, freight cars. If you had listed all the uses of flatcars you might have mentioned the way tanks were carried during the war, and in that way thought up the immensely profitable piggy-back system by which truck trailers are hauled on flat cars and then driven off for doorstep delivery.

Make up an idea museum. It can be catalogues of parts, models, or even pictures. For a fashion designer it might be fashions of the past; for a car designer, models of old-time autos. An upholstering company might have all sorts of materials from canvas to leather that its idea men could look at, touch, test, feel, tug.

The idea man who thinks up uses is as important as the one who invents products themselves. Charles Barbier, a French army officer, developed a system of night writing which made use of raised dots on paper. He designed it so his soldiers could read messages in the dark. It was a good idea, but the man who saw a new use for it changed the lives of thousands upon thousands of blind people. The man who saw that new use in 1829 was named Louis Braille.

John H. Patterson, founder of the National Cash Register Company, was walking through his Dayton plant years ago when he heard a worker complain that the foreman would take all the credit for any new ideas. Patterson remembered that when he had visited the Doge's Palace in Venice he had seen a slot in the wall where citizens used to drop in suggestions generations before. He had suggestion boxes put up in his Dayton plant, and today hundreds of companies in the United States follow his example.

Donald R. Brann and his wife bought an old house in Pleasantville, New York, in 1938. In making changes around the house he got the idea for drawing tissue paper patterns, just like dress patterns, for do-it-yourselfers. Since then he has turned out more than three million woodworking patterns for home fixer-uppers like himself.

One thing the brainstormer should do is divide his problem into its component parts. For example, the problem may not be a poorly operating television set but a poorly operating tube. Then if you look at the tube you may find it's not a poorly operating tube but a badly designed filament.

Now you have a specific problem: how to design a better filament.

But again you might break that problem into its parts. The design might not be bad. It might be the machine that makes it, or even the material that goes into it.

First, you have to find the proper problem, then you can brainstorm it.

One way to build an inventory of problems and solutions is carry an idea trap.

What's that? It's a pocket notebook you always carry with you so you can catch a fleeting idea on the wing—while you are stopped for a traffic light or riding the subway, eating lunch, waiting for a doctor's appointment, walking by a store window, or watching the World Series on television.

Some men even keep special idea traps in the bathroom, on their car dashboard, or have one by their bed that is equipped with a small battery lamp so ideas can be trapped efficiently in the dark of the night.

Willard Pleuthner, BBDO vice-president in charge of brainstorming, has said, "We should always have pencils and papers with us, no matter where we go. Especially at our bedside, because sometimes just before you go to sleep or just before you really wake up, your subconscious pours out to you ideas on problems that you have tucked back in that subconscious mind. . . . We should also take pencils and paper to church. Some people get their best ideas in church. That is not irreverent. I think the Lord gives us an extra reward for going to church. We are at peace with the world, and again that subconscious throws out ideas it has been working on."

The full-time brainstormer should make an idea bank where he makes deposits of ideas until the time is right to withdraw and invest them. There are all sorts of idea banks, ranging from file drawers to a small notebook. The important thing is to have a backlog or inventory of ideas arranged in some sort of order so that you can turn to them when you are trying to solve a problem.

Many companies today keep idea banks on an ornate scale. Clipping services are pasting more than twenty million clippings a year in corporate scrapbooks. The companies are paying five million dollars for this service so it must be paying off. Construction and engineering concerns keep clippings of proposed building jobs. A jail break may turn up a prospect for a lock company; a series of unusual fires, the idea for a special insurance policy; a list of accidents, the idea for a safety device.

Sometimes these idea banks can be turned directly into profits. For twenty years a newspaper rewrite man kept putting scraps of information about "The Day Lincoln Was Shot" in file folders. His name was Jim Bishop, and he wrote a fantastically successful book. H. L. Mencken once related: "Ever since my earliest attempts as an author I have followed the somewhat banal practice of setting down notions as they came to me . . . and then throwing these notes into a bin. Out of that bin have come a couple of dozen books and pamphlets and an almost innumerable swarm of magazine and newspaper articles, but still the raw materials kept mounting faster than I could work them up."

Conventions can be wonderfully inspiring sources for ideas. If you can't go to a convention and tour the exhibits, write and see if you can get transcripts of the speeches to peruse at your leisure.

Don't just go to your own convention; attend others as a visitor. A salesman can get ideas for new products and markets at a manufacturer's convention; a manufacturer can be stimulated by a bunch of scientists; and the scientists might come up with some new ideas if they spent several days with men who spend their time on the road, selling.

Seek out new experiences and new friends, join organizations, go to classes nights, travel to new places. To get ideas you must constantly be stimulated.

Take up painting. Your painting may be no good, but you will get a new appreciation of color and line; you will see a new world about you. Take a course or read a textbook on chemistry. Again you will broaden your understanding of the world.

Read the Congressional Record and special committee reports. They may be rough going, but they are often packed with facts.

Use every opportunity to talk to new people, see new places and things—and then come back to see the familiar with the eye of an explorer. The Compleat Brainstormer is a Renaissance Man who takes all knowledge to be his province.

SECRETS OF A SUCCESSFUL IDEA MAN

why you should give
ideas away

how to exercise
your subconscious

the importance of
having a deadline

why keep score
on yourself

how to make
your own wish book

what more ideas
would mean
to you

the basic secret of
all idea men

The real secret of a successful idea man is simple: He does something about his ideas.

Each of us has seen a new idea and said, "Why, I thought of that a year ago." We say it with scorn, but we should direct the scorn at ourselves, not at the person who had the drive to do something about it.

Successful idea men generate ideas all the time, and they don't hoard them. They do something about them, even if they give them away.

There are a lot of other satisfactions than money in doing this. When I give an idea away and see it acted upon, I get a great thrill of satisfaction and accomplishment. The important thing is to keep having ideas and to keep putting them to work.

Most of us are lazy, however. We mean to do better, to improve ourselves, to make this year better than last one. But we fall down, we forget, we drift.

There are ways we keep prodding ourselves into reaching farther, to going beyond ourselves. We must, just like an athlete, consciously exercise our brain cells. If we do this, we will be amazed at how our creative energies will increase.

The more we see, the more our powers of observation increase.

It is imperative that we push, goad, drive, spur ourselves into being more creative.

The more we look, the more we see. The more we think,

the more thoughts we have. The more combinations of ideas we try, the more combinations we realize are available. The more we practice the principles of problem-solving, the more problems we will solve.

Listen to H. W. Prentis, Jr., Chairman of the Board of Armstrong Cork: "To analyze and synthesize is not always easy, but here, as in most things, practice increases one's ability. It was interesting for me to watch myself develop to the point where I could tackle problems I could not possibly have handled a few years before. Unless a man tries, he cannot develop this capacity. In this business of taking things apart, there's hardly a week passes that something doesn't come up that seems just about insoluble, like a greased pole you cannot possibly climb. But if you keep at it long enough —keep the problem constantly before you—gradually you can break it down into its component parts, which you can grasp and solve."

I learned to exercise my creative powers several years ago when I read an article in the *Reader's Digest* which advised "Try Giving Yourself Away." I tried it.

My first attempt was a smashing failure, but I still found it was fun. I broke a shoelace one morning and couldn't find a substitute, so I sat right down and wrote a number of shoe manufacturers, suggesting they give a spare shoelace away with a new pair of shoes, or send a pair to a customer after six months. The idea didn't catch on, but I got a stack of amusing letters from shoe manufacturers for my troubles.

Later I was writing to a friend overseas. I wanted to send the letter airmail—the postage was high and rated by half-ounces, but I couldn't tell how much the onion-skin paper weighed. I wrote several paper manufacturers and got some action. I didn't get a free box of stationery, but I do have the satisfaction of walking into a stationery store or a Woolworth's and seeing the weight of the paper—one sheet, two, three, and so forth—printed on the bottom of the box of airmail stationery. I admit it gives me a real lift and feeling of accomplishment. This increases my motivation to do something about other ideas, bigger ideas. It boosts my confidence and makes me know that my ideas can be put to work, that someone will listen to it when I have one.

A bigger idea I'm much more proud of is the dial-a-prayer one. I read on the subway one night about a YMCA man in Baltimore who had an inspirational message which people could get by phoning a certain number. I was job hunting at the time, and I thought what a lift I would get if I could dial a number and get a Scripture reading or a prayer before going in to have an interview for a job. Then I thought of all the other times I needed a lift in a day full of the pressures of modern life.

I tried to get this done in New York but failed. I have since learned that the idea had struck other people, and that it was practiced on the West Coast. But I didn't know this, and a year or so afterward I tried again to get some action on this —and it caught on in New York City (Circle 6–4200). Today hundreds of churches have the service, and many churches have had to add numerous telephone numbers and tape-recording machines to keep up with the need. I know the dial-a-prayer idea helps people when they need help most, and I get a great deal of satisfaction out of the role I have played in it.

These are not revolutionary ideas and not even completely original ones. That is important. You have to start small, but once you put those relatively small ideas into circulation, you'll find you have more ideas and then still more. As they are adopted, you will double your confidence in presenting ideas. You will develop the habit of having ideas and doing something about them. You will build a backlog of laboratory experience in having ideas and selling them. All this increases what I call your CIQ, your creative initiative quotient.

Once you dare to be creative you will learn how much bigger your world has grown. C. Willard Bryant of General Electric, for example, has discovered, "We spend too much time endeavoring to remove 5 or 10 per cent of cost. It has been found that it is actually easier to remove 50 per cent of cost in many cases. This statement probably sounds like the most ridiculous one of the year. However, it is true, because while attempting to remove 50 per cent of the cost, we push out into the areas where no one else has thought improvement possible."

One of the best ways to keep ourselves moving ahead is to make a deadline. This is a basic working condition of newspapermen, and we should all understand just why and how it works.

Reporters and editors, just like all of us, procrastinate. The job of reporting never ends. There is always more information to get, more people to interview, more clippings to read, more phone calls to make. But there is always the deadline. At that time copy has to be on its way through the editing process and on its way to be set in type. Because of the deadline the reporter has to stop and start writing.

When he writes he again can find plenty of reasons to delay the final version. He needs to clean his typewriter, get uncreased copy paper, new carbons. He has to try a new lead again and again, sharpen up a sentence, check a quote. But once more the deadline stares him in the face. There is a time when he has to do a job, not just get ready to do it. It might have been a better job if he had longer, but for better or for worse, he has to do his job—and many times the most brilliant jobs of writing have been done under the most difficult deadlines.

As the reporter moves into other fields, he may find his daily deadline changed, but he will find he still has a deadline. It may be a weekly magazine deadline or a monthly one; it may become an hourly one if he works for a radio news broadcast, or it may stretch to a yearly one or a three-yearly one if he writes books. But eventually will come the moment of truth when he must sit down before some blank paper and produce a product. There is always that deadline saying, "Ready or not, here I come."

We can all learn a lesson from the newspaper deadline, and we should set one for ourselves. It shouldn't be so tight we can't keep it and become depressed by the impossible goal, but it should be tight enough to keep us moving, to keep us stretching our faculties.

Once we have established this deadline—for example, in a month I'm going to have that shipping problem licked, by the end of the year I'm going to have a promotion—then we should make it impossible for ourselves to forget it.

There are a number of ways to do this. We can mark up a desk calendar or a wall calendar—better still: both. We should not only mark down the deadline but steps along the way. For example, a notation might read, "Are you halfway finished on that marketing report?" We should always keep reminding ourselves in the manner of the advertisements which say, "Only thirty-five shopping days to Christmas," that we have only thirty-five more working days until we promised ourselves we'd come up with a new idea for the boss.

Often we can prod ourselves by making our secretaries remind us. Some men tape a card with the deadline date on the sun visor in their car so they will see it when they least expect it—when they turn the visor down. There are even men who leave a note to themselves in their hat or give their wives a letter to be mailed to them in three weeks or three months when they may have forgotten all about their deadline.

Frank Tibolt, a pioneer teacher in Philadelphia of creativity, tells this story:

> *Ivy Lee used to operate an efficiency firm in New York. His regular clients were Rockefeller, Morgan, the Du Ponts, Pennsylvania Railroad, and other giant corporations.*
>
> *One day, Lee called on Schwab of the Bethlehem Steel Company. Lee outlined briefly his firm's services, ending with the statement: "With our service, you'll know how to manage better." "Hell," said Schwab. "I'm not managing as well now as I know how. What we need around here is not more 'knowing' but more 'doing'; not knowledge but action. If you can give us something to pep us up to do the things we already know we ought to do, I'll gladly listen to you and pay you anything you ask."*

"Fine," said Lee. "I can give you something in twenty minutes that will step up your 'action' and 'doing' at least fifty per cent."

"O.K.," said Schwab. "I have just about that much time before I must leave to catch a train. What's your idea?"

Lee pulled a blank 3-by-5 note sheet out of his pocket, handed it to Schwab and said: "Write on this sheet the six most important tasks you have to do tomorrow." That took about three minutes. "Now," said Lee, "number them in the order of their importance." Five more minutes passed. "Now," said Lee, "put this sheet in your pocket and the first thing tomorrow morning look at item one and start working on it. Pull the sheet out of your pocket every fifteen minutes and look at item one until it's finished. Then tackle item two in the same way, then item three. Do this until quitting time. Don't be concerned if you only finish two or three or even if you only finish one item. You'll be working on the important ones. The others can wait. If you can't finish them all by this method, you couldn't with any other method, either, and without some system you'd probably not even decide which are most important.

"Spend the last five minutes of every working day making out a 'must' list for the next day's tasks. After you've convinced yourself of the worth of this system, have your men try it. Try it out as long as you wish and then send me a check for what you think it's worth."

The whole interview lasted about twenty-five minutes. In two weeks Schwab sent Lee a check for twenty-five thousand dollars—a thousand dollars a minute. He added a note saying the lesson was the most profitable from a *money standpoint he ever learned. Did it work? In five years it turned the unknown Bethlehem Steel Company into the biggest independent steel producer in the world; made Schwab a hundred-million-dollar fortune and the best known steel man alive at that time.*

There are all sorts of ways to force yourself into working, into turning your ideas into acts. Self-starting is a problem faced by people in all sorts of lines of work. But it is a problem that can be licked.

Some writers stop writing before they run out of ideas, so that the pump is primed for the next day, others just put anything down on paper—doggerel, notes, anything to get them writing until the work really starts to flow. One executive breaks the big jobs down into small chunks of work he can handle while always seeing the end in sight.

One thing a successful idea man must realize is his power. He not only knows how important ideas are, he knows that ideas are a force which can influence the largest corporations, the most moribund organizations. Some idea men keep before them a score card of what they have accomplished, to encourage them to do more things.

At the same time he realizes that there is not only a need for big ideas, for truly creative ideas which will radically change our company or even our world, but for small ideas which we can all have, new combinations and variations of ideas.

There are many ways to motivate yourself so that you will keep working. Fit the goal to your own situation and personality. One man wanted to go to England, so he put a map on the wall, and for each dollar he saved he drew a line a bit longer on the map. He could really see where he was going. He made a wish book, pasting pictures of England, life on shipboard, travel clothes, and so forth, to remind him of his goal.

One of the most successful sales managers of the Avon Company tells her saleswomen to cut out a picture of what they are working for—a home, or a car, or a college education for her children, and paste it on her mirror so each day she will be motivated to work hard toward that goal.

Perhaps you have to see what you are working for. Here is a selected list from a brainstorm I held on WHAT WOULD YOU GAIN IF YOU COULD THINK UP MORE IDEAS?

> *Job promotion.*
> *Make more money.*
> *Could think of something that might have commercial value —patentable ideas.*
> *Recognition from company as fellow with lots of "good" ideas.*
> *Satisfaction achieved through creation.*
> *Feeling of pride—self-satisfaction in thinking of something new and seeing it put into use.*
> *Would have a more satisfactory life generally—be able to solve problems at home and at work better.*
> *Make a better contribution to community activities in which I participate.*
> *Find easier ways of doing work.*
> *Development of an entirely new field for my company.*
> *Would be a better help to boss, who may not have time to generate ideas.*

Make a list of what you want to do with your life, of all your dreams. I had everyone do this at the University of

Akron Creative Thinking Institute and found out that no one had any trouble quickly writing down a number of dreams. They ran the gamut of human behavior. "I'm going to take golf lessons, get married, build my own house, go back to college, learn to play the banjo, get a better job, take a trip to Hawaii, retire, diet, go into church work full time, run for Congress." Then I had the same people write down something they could do to put their dream to work the very next morning. It might be starting a special savings account, enrolling in school, proposing to your girl, talking to your minister, filing primary papers, eating less for lunch, buying a banjo. The point is that you can act, right now, today, to make your dreams come true. Tomorrow is now.

That's the final secret of all successful idea men. They know that right now is the time to have ideas and right now is the time to do something about them. Brainstorm ways in which to make your dreams come true. Stop right here and brainstorm them—then go out and start working toward that goal. Not tomorrow, but today.

AMERICA'S LAST FRONTIER

*one man's
creative adventure*

*what you can do
with your own ideas*

*the most important
revolution
of our age*

*what it can mean
to your future*

*how you can be
a pioneer
in creativity,
our last frontier*

It was a Saturday night in 1948. I had no plans as I strolled along Market Street in Philadelphia with that special feeling of loneliness that only Saturday night can give you. By accident I wandered into a store and found a book which changed my whole life.

At the time I was a sales demonstrator for the Philadelphia Electric Company. I was twenty-eight years old and making seventy-six dollars a week. I kept hoping that my ship would come in, but it didn't. Every time the alumni magazine arrived I felt myself slipping far behind the other members of my Harvard class. My Walter Mitty-like dreams just weren't coming true, and I couldn't find much satisfaction in dreaming them any more.

Then I bought that book. It was *Your Creative Power* by Alex Osborn. I went right home and stayed up until 2 A.M. reading it. What was more important, I started living it.

The next morning I decided to call Alex Osborn long distance in Buffalo to discuss the book. Before I went into the pay phone in the corner drugstore I walked around the block, once, twice, three times. Who was I, an appliance demonstrator, to call the head of one of the world's largest advertising agencies on Sunday morning? Yet I had taken his book to heart. I did call him, and started a new life.

Eventually I took my master's degree at the University of Pennsylvania. I worked with Alex Osborn and then I went ahead on my own to build a career in creativity. At times I had difficulty supporting myself while trying to sell creative thinking to industry. Once when my picture was in *Fortune* magazine I was actually living in a YMCA and working as a Good Humor man.

I have come a long way from that lonely Saturday night on Market Street. I have an apartment just off Park Avenue in midtown Manhatten. My office is in one of New York City's most beautiful office buildings. I have been sent all over the country, even overseas by one of the nation's largest corporations. I have had a wonderful creative adventure because I acted on my ideas.

I tell this story only because it should inspire you. No one had less on the ball than I did that Saturday night in Philadelphia.

I have become convinced by my own experience that man is not a marionette of fate, that he can make a difference in his life and eventually a difference in his world.

First he has to learn how to have ideas.

Then he has to know how to promote them.

If he realizes but a portion of his potentialities, there is no limit to his future.

This is true because we are involved in a great revolution. A revolution which has created America's newest frontier, where we can all find opportunity, new resources, a fresh chance, a challenge. It is the frontier of creativity.

Until our century creative thinking was the private estate of a few men. Most of the inventions which led up to our modern world were developed by pure and unadulterated chance.

In the past fifty years, however, there came a development

which attempted to eliminate this element of chance. We put the scientific method to work in great research laboratories, which organized knowledge into narrow fields and made its explorers specialists, Ph.D.'s with many years of advanced study. This work will still go on, and it should.

But now to supplement that effort we have a new emphasis on creative thinking. We have discovered how everyone, with formal education or without it, can attack his problems creatively. The principles of creative thinking can be taught. We can all brainstorm the problems of our world.

In our democracy we are blessed with the freedom to own property, the freedom to vote, the freedom to worship, the freedom to receive an education. We have the freedom to think creatively, to have ideas, and most important, the freedom to express them.

This is our new frontier, and we desperately need pioneers to explore that frontier and develop its resources before it is too late. This is your mission.

This revolution has come none too soon. The march of Christianity, of all that is good in Western and Eastern culture, in fact the progress of man depends on the strength of our ideas.

The Bomb has made it essential that we have the political, economical, and religious-philosophical ideas which will make it possible for man to live in peace with man.

Our world is becoming smaller and smaller. We have extended life, and we must learn how to support that life and make better use of it. We need more resources, especially that vital resource that exists only in our minds.

Not long ago a team of scientists from the California Institute of Technology looked at our world a hundred years from now, our children's children's world.

They saw two to four times as large a population, two to four times as many mouths to feed, yet they saw no want; instead, a great machine civilization making use of every resource. This could come about, they reported, *if* we develop the brain power to design and run this great global technological civilization.

They cited as our greatest problem the development of brain power. They gave high priority to developing much further the creative brain power of women, who make up half our population but one per cent of our engineers; to realizing the full benefit of the brains which are imprisoned in minority groups; to salvaging the two thirds of our highly intelligent youths who do not get advanced education and who never utilize their intelligence in their life work.

That study was but one of many which has emphasized this need for increased brain power. Leaders in all fields have dramatized how much we need the full potentialities of the human brain.

Crawford H. Greenewalt, president of Du Pont, in a speech called "Key to Progress—the Uncommon Man" has said, "Just when we will realize (the) promise of the future and how far the new developments will take us depends on how well we are able to recognize and encourage individual achievement. We cannot move very rapidly if we shut the door on our ablest people by absorbing them in the lifeless tomb of mediocrity. . . .

"Try as we will, we can create no synthetic genius, no composite leader. Men are not interchangeable parts like so many pinion gears or carburetors; genius, as John Adams said, is bestowed 'imperiously' by nature upon an individual. And behind every advance of the human race is a germ of creation growing in the mind of some lone individual, an individual whose dreams waken him in the night while others lie contentedly asleep.

"We need those dreams, for today's dreams represent tomorrow's realities. Yet, in the very nature of our mass effort, there lies this grave danger—not that the individual may circumvent the public will, but that he will himself be conformed and shaped to the general pattern, with the loss of his unique, original contributions. The group nature of business enterprise itself will provide adequate safeguards against public affront. The great problem, the great question, is to develop within the framework of the group the creative genius of the individual.

"It is a problem for management, for public education, for government, for the church, for the press—for everyone. The stake is both the material one of preserving our most productive source of progress and the spiritual one of insuring to each individual the human dignity which is his birthright.

"I know of no problem so pressing, of no issue so vital. For unless we can guarantee the encouragement and fruitfulness of the uncommon man, the future will lose for all men its virtue, its brightness, and its promise."

Brainstorming is one way we can discover the uncommon man and his ideas. It can help solve the great problems of life. It can be used to solve the vast problems of science, of government, of philosophy.

Most of us use only a fraction of our brain power. We can

no longer afford that great waste. We must learn how to mobilize all our creative force to solve the fundamental problems of our world.

This, then, is the mission and the charge to each of us: we must develop our own creativity and our own subconscious, so that we can make a telling contribution to the progress of our civilization.

In learning how to do this, we shall all be explorers of an area that is hardly known.

No one yet really knows how the mind functions, why it is so very much more than a giant computer reduced to portable size. Each of us can, however, probe the limits of this world.

This book is not an end. It is a summing up of the present art of brainstorming, but it is a beginning and an inspiration to discover what we can do with our brain power to make our world a better one.

Try brainstorming—and find out how to think up ideas that make a difference in your life and our world.

A PERSONAL WORD FROM MELVIN POWERS, PUBLISHER, WILSHIRE BOOK COMPANY

My goal is to publish interesting, informative, and inspirational books. You can help me to accomplish this by sending me your answers to the following questions:

Did you enjoy reading this book? Why?

What ideas in the book impressed you most? Have you applied them to your daily life? How?

Is there a chapter that could serve as a theme for an entire book? Explain.

Would you like to read similar books? What additional information would you like them to contain?

If you have an idea for a book, I would welcome discussing it with you. If you have a manuscript in progress, write or call me concerning possible publication.

Melvin Powers
12015 Sherman Road
North Hollywood, California 91605

(818) 765-8579

MELVIN POWERS SELF-IMPROVEMENT LIBRARY

ASTROLOGY

____ ASTROLOGY: HOW TO CHART YOUR HOROSCOPE *Max Heindel*	5.00
____ ASTROLOGY AND SEXUAL ANALYSIS *Morris C. Goodman*	5.00
____ ASTROLOGY AND YOU *Carroll Righter*	5.00
____ ASTROLOGY MADE EASY *Astarte*	5.00
____ ASTROLOGY, ROMANCE, YOU AND THE STARS *Anthony Norvell*	5.00
____ MY WORLD OF ASTROLOGY *Sydney Omarr*	7.00
____ THOUGHT DIAL *Sydney Omarr*	7.00
____ WHAT THE STARS REVEAL ABOUT THE MEN IN YOUR LIFE *Thelma White*	3.00

BRIDGE

____ BRIDGE BIDDING MADE EASY *Edwin B. Kantar*	10.00
____ BRIDGE CONVENTIONS *Edwin B. Kantar*	10.00
____ COMPETITIVE BIDDING IN MODERN BRIDGE *Edgar Kaplan*	7.00
____ DEFENSIVE BRIDGE PLAY COMPLETE *Edwin B. Kantar*	15.00
____ GAMESMAN BRIDGE—PLAY BETTER WITH KANTAR *Edwin B. Kantar*	7.00
____ HOW TO IMPROVE YOUR BRIDGE *Alfred Sheinwold*	7.00
____ IMPROVING YOUR BIDDING SKILLS *Edwin B. Kantar*	7.00
____ INTRODUCTION TO DECLARER'S PLAY *Edwin B. Kantar*	7.00
____ INTRODUCTION TO DEFENDER'S PLAY *Edwin B. Kantar*	7.00
____ KANTAR FOR THE DEFENSE *Edwin B. Kantar*	7.00
____ KANTAR FOR THE DEFENSE VOLUME 2 *Edwin B. Kantar*	7.00
____ TEST YOUR BRIDGE PLAY *Edwin B. Kantar*	7.00
____ VOLUME 2—TEST YOUR BRIDGE PLAY *Edwin B. Kantar*	7.00
____ WINNING DECLARER PLAY *Dorothy Hayden Truscott*	10.00

BUSINESS, STUDY & REFERENCE

____ BRAINSTORMING *Charles Clark*	10.00
____ CONVERSATION MADE EASY *Elliot Russell*	5.00
____ EXAM SECRET *Dennis B. Jackson*	5.00
____ FIX-IT BOOK *Arthur Symons*	2.00
____ HOW TO DEVELOP A BETTER SPEAKING VOICE *M. Hellier*	5.00
____ HOW TO SAVE 50% ON GAS & CAR EXPENSES *Ken Stansbie*	5.00
____ HOW TO SELF-PUBLISH YOUR BOOK & MAKE IT A BEST SELLER *Melvin Powers*	20.00
____ INCREASE YOUR LEARNING POWER *Geoffrey A. Dudley*	5.00
____ PRACTICAL GUIDE TO BETTER CONCENTRATION *Melvin Powers*	5.00
____ 7 DAYS TO FASTER READING *William S. Schaill*	7.00
____ SONGWRITERS' RHYMING DICTIONARY *Jane Shaw Whitfield*	10.00
____ SPELLING MADE EASY *Lester D. Basch & Dr. Milton Finkelstein*	3.00
____ STUDENT'S GUIDE TO BETTER GRADES *J. A. Rickard*	3.00
____ TEST YOURSELF—FIND YOUR HIDDEN TALENT *Jack Shafer*	3.00
____ YOUR WILL & WHAT TO DO ABOUT IT *Attorney Samuel G. Kling*	5.00

CALLIGRAPHY

____ ADVANCED CALLIGRAPHY *Katherine Jeffares*	7.00
____ CALLIGRAPHY—THE ART OF BEAUTIFUL WRITING *Katherine Jeffares*	7.00
____ CALLIGRAPHY FOR FUN & PROFIT *Anne Leptich & Jacque Evans*	7.00
____ CALLIGRAPHY MADE EASY *Tina Serafini*	7.00

CHESS & CHECKERS

____ BEGINNER'S GUIDE TO WINNING CHESS *Fred Reinfeld*	7.00
____ CHESS IN TEN EASY LESSONS *Larry Evans*	5.00
____ CHESS MADE EASY *Milton L. Hanauer*	5.00
____ CHESS PROBLEMS FOR BEGINNERS *Edited by Fred Reinfeld*	5.00
____ CHESS TACTICS FOR BEGINNERS *Edited by Fred Reinfeld*	5.00

____ HOW TO WIN AT CHECKERS *Fred Reinfeld*		5.00
____ 1001 BRILLIANT WAYS TO CHECKMATE *Fred Reinfeld*		10.00
____ 1001 WINNING CHESS SACRIFICES & COMBINATIONS *Fred Reinfeld*		7.00

COOKERY & HERBS

____ CULPEPER'S HERBAL REMEDIES *Dr. Nicholas Culpeper*	5.00
____ FAST GOURMET COOKBOOK *Poppy Cannon*	2.50
____ HEALING POWER OF HERBS *May Bethel*	5.00
____ HEALING POWER OF NATURAL FOODS *May Bethel*	7.00
____ HERBS FOR HEALTH—HOW TO GROW & USE THEM *Louise Evans Doole*	5.00
____ HOME GARDEN COOKBOOK—DELICIOUS NATURAL FOOD RECIPES *Ken Kraft*	3.00
____ MEATLESS MEAL GUIDE *Tomi Ryan & James H. Ryan, M.D.*	4.00
____ VEGETABLE GARDENING FOR BEGINNERS *Hugh Wiberg*	2.00
____ VEGETABLES FOR TODAY'S GARDENS *R. Milton Carleton*	2.00
____ VEGETARIAN COOKERY *Janet Walker*	7.00
____ VEGETARIAN COOKING MADE EASY & DELECTABLE *Veronica Vezza*	3.00
____ VEGETARIAN DELIGHTS—A HAPPY COOKBOOK FOR HEALTH *K. R. Mehta*	2.00

GAMBLING & POKER

____ HOW TO WIN AT DICE GAMES *Skip Frey*	3.00
____ HOW TO WIN AT POKER *Terence Reese & Anthony T. Watkins*	7.00
____ SCARNE ON DICE *John Scarne*	15.00
____ WINNING AT CRAPS *Dr. Lloyd T. Commins*	5.00
____ WINNING AT GIN *Chester Wander & Cy Rice*	3.00
____ WINNING AT POKER—AN EXPERT'S GUIDE *John Archer*	5.00
____ WINNING AT 21—AN EXPERT'S GUIDE *John Archer*	7.00
____ WINNING POKER SYSTEMS *Norman Zadeh*	3.00

HEALTH

____ BEE POLLEN *Lynda Lyngheim & Jack Scagnetti*	5.00
____ COPING WITH ALZHEIMER'S *Rose Oliver, Ph.D. & Francis Bock, Ph.D.*	10.00
____ DR. LINDNER'S POINT SYSTEM FOOD PROGRAM *Peter G. Lindner, M.D.*	2.00
____ HELP YOURSELF TO BETTER SIGHT *Margaret Darst Corbett*	7.00
____ HOW YOU CAN STOP SMOKING PERMANENTLY *Ernest Caldwell*	5.00
____ MIND OVER PLATTER *Peter G. Lindner, M.D.*	5.00
____ NATURE'S WAY TO NUTRITION & VIBRANT HEALTH *Robert J. Scrutton*	3.00
____ NEW CARBOHYDRATE DIET COUNTER *Patti Lopez-Pereira*	2.00
____ REFLEXOLOGY *Dr. Maybelle Segal*	5.00
____ REFLEXOLOGY FOR GOOD HEALTH *Anna Kaye & Don C. Matchan*	7.00
____ 30 DAYS TO BEAUTIFUL LEGS *Dr. Marc Selner*	3.00
____ WONDER WITHIN *Thomas F. Coyle, M.D.*	10.00
____ YOU CAN LEARN TO RELAX *Dr. Samuel Gutwirth*	5.00

HOBBIES

____ BEACHCOMBING FOR BEGINNERS *Norman Hickin*	2.00
____ BLACKSTONE'S MODERN CARD TRICKS *Harry Blackstone*	7.00
____ BLACKSTONE'S SECRETS OF MAGIC *Harry Blackstone*	5.00
____ COIN COLLECTING FOR BEGINNERS *Burton Hobson & Fred Reinfeld*	7.00
____ ENTERTAINING WITH ESP *Tony 'Doc' Shiels*	2.00
____ 400 FASCINATING MAGIC TRICKS YOU CAN DO *Howard Thurston*	7.00
____ HOW I TURN JUNK INTO FUN AND PROFIT *Sari*	3.00
____ HOW TO WRITE A HIT SONG & SELL IT *Tommy Boyce*	10.00
____ MAGIC FOR ALL AGES *Walter Gibson*	4.00
____ STAMP COLLECTING FOR BEGINNERS *Burton Hobson*	3.00

HORSE PLAYER'S WINNING GUIDES

____ BETTING HORSES TO WIN *Les Conklin*	7.00
____ ELIMINATE THE LOSERS *Bob McKnight*	5.00
____ HOW TO PICK WINNING HORSES *Bob McKnight*	5.00

___ HOW TO WIN AT THE RACES *Sam (The Genius) Lewin*	5.00
___ HOW YOU CAN BEAT THE RACES *Jack Kavanaqh*	5.00
___ MAKING MONEY AT THE RACES *David Barr*	5.00
___ PAYDAY AT THE RACES *Les Conklin*	5.00
___ SMART HANDICAPPING MADE EASY *William Bauman*	5.00
___ SUCCESS AT THE HARNESS RACES *Barry Meadow*	5.00

HUMOR

___ HOW TO FLATTEN YOUR TUSH *Coach Marge Reardon*	2.00
___ JOKE TELLER'S HANDBOOK *Bob Orben*	7.00
___ JOKES FOR ALL OCCASIONS *Al Schock*	5.00
___ 2,000 NEW LAUGHS FOR SPEAKERS *Bob Orben*	7.00
___ 2,400 JOKES TO BRIGHTEN YOUR SPEECHES *Robert Orben*	7.00
___ 2,500 JOKES TO START 'EM LAUGHING *Bob Orben*	7.00

HYPNOTISM

___ ADVANCED TECHNIQUES OF HYPNOSIS *Melvin Powers*	3.00
___ CHILDBIRTH WITH HYPNOSIS *William S. Kroger, M.D.*	5.00
___ HOW TO SOLVE YOUR SEX PROBLEMS WITH SELF-HYPNOSIS *Frank S. Caprio, M.D.*	5.00
___ HOW TO STOP SMOKING THRU SELF-HYPNOSIS *Leslie M. LeCron*	3.00
___ HOW YOU CAN BOWL BETTER USING SELF-HYPNOSIS *Jack Heise*	4.00
___ HOW YOU CAN PLAY BETTER GOLF USING SELF-HYPNOSIS *Jack Heise*	3.00
___ HYPNOSIS AND SELF-HYPNOSIS *Bernard Hollander, M.D.*	5.00
___ HYPNOTISM *(Originally published in 1893) Carl Sextus*	5.00
___ HYPNOTISM MADE EASY *Dr. Ralph Winn*	5.00
___ HYPNOTISM MADE PRACTICAL *Louis Orton*	5.00
___ HYPNOTISM REVEALED *Melvin Powers*	3.00
___ HYPNOTISM TODAY *Leslie LeCron and Jean Bordeaux, Ph.D.*	5.00
___ MODERN HYPNOSIS *Lesley Kuhn & Salvatore Russo, Ph.D.*	5.00
___ NEW CONCEPTS OF HYPNOSIS *Bernard C. Gindes, M.D.*	10.00
___ NEW SELF-HYPNOSIS *Paul Adams*	7.00
___ POST-HYPNOTIC INSTRUCTIONS—SUGGESTIONS FOR THERAPY *Arnold Furst*	10.00
___ PRACTICAL GUIDE TO SELF-HYPNOSIS *Melvin Powers*	5.00
___ PRACTICAL HYPNOTISM *Philip Magonet, M.D.*	3.00
___ SECRETS OF HYPNOTISM *S. J. Van Pelt, M.D.*	5.00
___ SELF-HYPNOSIS—A CONDITIONED-RESPONSE TECHNIQUE *Laurence Sparks*	7.00
___ SELF-HYPNOSIS—ITS THEORY, TECHNIQUE & APPLICATION *Melvin Powers*	3.00
___ THERAPY THROUGH HYPNOSIS *Edited by Raphael H. Rhodes*	5.00

JUDAICA

___ SERVICE OF THE HEART *Evelyn Garfiel, Ph.D.*	10.00
___ STORY OF ISRAEL IN COINS *Jean & Maurice Gould*	2.00
___ STORY OF ISRAEL IN STAMPS *Maxim & Gabriel Shamir*	1.00
___ TONGUE OF THE PROPHETS *Robert St. John*	7.00

JUST FOR WOMEN

___ COSMOPOLITAN'S GUIDE TO MARVELOUS MEN *Foreword by Helen Gurley Brown*	3.00
___ COSMOPOLITAN'S HANG-UP HANDBOOK *Foreword by Helen Gurley Brown*	4.00
___ COSMOPOLITAN'S LOVE BOOK—A GUIDE TO ECSTASY IN BED	7.00
___ COSMOPOLITAN'S NEW ETIQUETTE GUIDE *Foreword by Helen Gurley Brown*	4.00
___ I AM A COMPLEAT WOMAN *Doris Hagopian & Karen O'Connor Sweeney*	3.00
___ JUST FOR WOMEN—A GUIDE TO THE FEMALE BODY *Richard E. Sand, M.D.*	5.00
___ NEW APPROACHES TO SEX IN MARRIAGE *John E. Eichenlaub, M.D.*	3.00
___ SEXUALLY ADEQUATE FEMALE *Frank S. Caprio, M.D.*	3.00
___ SEXUALLY FULFILLED WOMAN *Dr. Rachel Copelan*	5.00

MARRIAGE, SEX & PARENTHOOD

____	ABILITY TO LOVE *Dr. Allan Fromme*	7.00
____	GUIDE TO SUCCESSFUL MARRIAGE *Drs. Albert Ellis & Robert Harper*	7.00
____	HOW TO RAISE AN EMOTIONALLY HEALTHY, HAPPY CHILD *Albert Ellis, Ph.D.*	10.00
____	PARENT SURVIVAL TRAINING *Marvin Silverman, Ed.D. & David Lustig, Ph.D.*	10.00
____	SEX WITHOUT GUILT *Albert Ellis, Ph.D.*	5.00
____	SEXUALLY ADEQUATE MALE *Frank S. Caprio, M.D.*	3.00
____	SEXUALLY FULFILLED MAN *Dr. Rachel Copelan*	5.00
____	STAYING IN LOVE *Dr. Norton F. Kristy*	7.00

MELVIN POWERS' MAIL ORDER LIBRARY

____	HOW TO GET RICH IN MAIL ORDER *Melvin Powers*	20.00
____	HOW TO SELF-PUBLISH YOUR BOOK & MAKE IT A BEST SELLER *Melvin Powers*	20.00
____	HOW TO WRITE A GOOD ADVERTISEMENT *Victor O. Schwab*	20.00
____	MAIL ORDER MADE EASY *J. Frank Brumbaugh*	20.00

METAPHYSICS & OCCULT

____	CONCENTRATION—A GUIDE TO MENTAL MASTERY *Mouni Sadhu*	7.00
____	EXTRA-TERRESTRIAL INTELLIGENCE—THE FIRST ENCOUNTER	6.00
____	FORTUNE TELLING WITH CARDS *P. Foli*	5.00
____	HOW TO INTERPRET DREAMS, OMENS & FORTUNE TELLING SIGNS *Gettings*	5.00
____	HOW TO UNDERSTAND YOUR DREAMS *Geoffrey A. Dudley*	5.00
____	IN DAYS OF GREAT PEACE *Mouni Sadhu*	3.00
____	MAGICIAN—HIS TRAINING AND WORK *W. E. Butler*	7.00
____	MEDITATION *Mouni Sadhu*	10.00
____	MODERN NUMEROLOGY *Morris C. Goodman*	5.00
____	NUMEROLOGY—ITS FACTS AND SECRETS *Ariel Yvon Taylor*	5.00
____	NUMEROLOGY MADE EASY *W. Mykian*	5.00
____	PALMISTRY MADE EASY *Fred Gettings*	5.00
____	PALMISTRY MADE PRACTICAL *Elizabeth Daniels Squire*	7.00
____	PROPHECY IN OUR TIME *Martin Ebon*	2.50
____	SUPERSTITION—ARE YOU SUPERSTITIOUS? *Eric Maple*	2.00
____	TAROT *Mouni Sadhu*	10.00
____	TAROT OF THE BOHEMIANS *Papus*	7.00
____	WAYS TO SELF-REALIZATION *Mouni Sadhu*	7.00
____	WITCHCRAFT, MAGIC & OCCULTISM—A FASCINATING HISTORY *W. B. Crow*	10.00
____	WITCHCRAFT—THE SIXTH SENSE *Justine Glass*	7.00

RECOVERY

____	KNIGHT IN RUSTY ARMOR *Robert Fisher*	5.00
____	KNIGHT IN RUSTY ARMOR *Robert Fisher (Hard cover edition)*	10.00

SELF-HELP & INSPIRATIONAL

____	CHARISMA—HOW TO GET "THAT SPECIAL MAGIC" *Marcia Grad*	7.00
____	DAILY POWER FOR JOYFUL LIVING *Dr. Donald Curtis*	7.00
____	DYNAMIC THINKING *Melvin Powers*	5.00
____	GREATEST POWER IN THE UNIVERSE *U. S. Andersen*	7.00
____	GROW RICH WHILE YOU SLEEP *Ben Sweetland*	8.00
____	GROW RICH WITH YOUR MILLION DOLLAR MIND *Brian Adams*	7.00
____	GROWTH THROUGH REASON *Albert Ellis, Ph.D.*	7.00
____	GUIDE TO PERSONAL HAPPINESS *Albert Ellis, Ph.D. & Irving Becker, Ed.D.*	7.00
____	HANDWRITING ANALYSIS MADE EASY *John Marley*	7.00
____	HANDWRITING TELLS *Nadya Olyanova*	7.00
____	HOW TO ATTRACT GOOD LUCK *A.H.Z. Carr*	7.00
____	HOW TO DEVELOP A WINNING PERSONALITY *Martin Panzer*	7.00
____	HOW TO DEVELOP AN EXCEPTIONAL MEMORY *Young & Gibson*	7.00
____	HOW TO LIVE WITH A NEUROTIC *Albert Ellis, Ph.D.*	7.00
____	HOW TO OVERCOME YOUR FEARS *M. P. Leahy, M.D.*	3.00
____	HOW TO SUCCEED *Brian Adams*	7.00

___ HUMAN PROBLEMS & HOW TO SOLVE THEM *Dr. Donald Curtis*	5.00
___ I CAN *Ben Sweetland*	8.00
___ I WILL *Ben Sweetland*	8.00
___ KNIGHT IN RUSTY ARMOR *Robert Fisher*	5.00
___ KNIGHT IN RUSTY ARMOR *Robert Fisher (Hard cover edition)*	10.00
___ LEFT-HANDED PEOPLE *Michael Barsley*	5.00
___ MAGIC IN YOUR MIND *U.S. Andersen*	10.00
___ MAGIC OF THINKING SUCCESS *Dr. David J. Schwartz*	8.00
___ MAGIC POWER OF YOUR MIND *Walter M. Germain*	7.00
___ MENTAL POWER THROUGH SLEEP SUGGESTION *Melvin Powers*	3.00
___ NEVER UNDERESTIMATE THE SELLING POWER OF A WOMAN *Dottie Walters*	7.00
___ NEW GUIDE TO RATIONAL LIVING *Albert Ellis, Ph.D. & R. Harper, Ph.D.*	7.00
___ PSYCHO-CYBERNETICS *Maxwell Maltz, M.D.*	7.00
___ PSYCHOLOGY OF HANDWRITING *Nadya Olyanova*	7.00
___ SALES CYBERNETICS *Brian Adams*	10.00
___ SCIENCE OF MIND IN DAILY LIVING *Dr. Donald Curtis*	7.00
___ SECRET OF SECRETS *U.S. Andersen*	7.00
___ SECRET POWER OF THE PYRAMIDS *U. S. Andersen*	7.00
___ SELF-THERAPY FOR THE STUTTERER *Malcolm Frazer*	3.00
___ SUCCESS-CYBERNETICS *U. S. Andersen*	7.00
___ 10 DAYS TO A GREAT NEW LIFE *William E. Edwards*	3.00
___ THINK AND GROW RICH *Napoleon Hill*	8.00
___ THINK LIKE A WINNER *Dr. Walter Doyle Staples*	10.00
___ THREE MAGIC WORDS *U. S. Andersen*	7.00
___ TREASURY OF COMFORT *Edited by Rabbi Sidney Greenberg*	10.00
___ TREASURY OF THE ART OF LIVING *Sidney S. Greenberg*	7.00
___ WHAT YOUR HANDWRITING REVEALS *Albert E. Hughes*	4.00
___ WONDER WITHIN *Thomas F. Coyle, M.D.*	10.00
___ YOUR SUBCONSCIOUS POWER *Charles M. Simmons*	7.00
___ YOUR THOUGHTS CAN CHANGE YOUR LIFE *Dr. Donald Curtis*	7.00

SPORTS

___ BILLIARDS—POCKET • CAROM • THREE CUSHION *Clive Cottingham, Jr.*	5.00
___ COMPLETE GUIDE TO FISHING *Vlad Evanoff*	2.00
___ HOW TO IMPROVE YOUR RACQUETBALL *Lubarsky, Kaufman & Scagnetti*	5.00
___ HOW TO WIN AT POCKET BILLIARDS *Edward D. Knuchell*	10.00
___ JOY OF WALKING *Jack Scagnetti*	3.00
___ LEARNING & TEACHING SOCCER SKILLS *Eric Worthington*	3.00
___ MOTORCYCLING FOR BEGINNERS *I.G. Edmonds*	3.00
___ RACQUETBALL FOR WOMEN *Toni Hudson, Jack Scagnetti & Vince Rondone*	3.00
___ SECRET OF BOWLING STRIKES *Dawson Taylor*	5.00
___ SOCCER—THE GAME & HOW TO PLAY IT *Gary Rosenthal*	7.00
___ STARTING SOCCER *Edward F. Dolan, Jr.*	3.00

TENNIS LOVER'S LIBRARY

___ HOW TO BEAT BETTER TENNIS PLAYERS *Loring Fiske*	4.00
___ PSYCH YOURSELF TO BETTER TENNIS *Dr. Walter A. Luszki*	2.00
___ TENNIS FOR BEGINNERS *Dr. H. A. Murray*	2.00
___ TENNIS MADE EASY *Joel Brecheen*	5.00
___ WEEKEND TENNIS—HOW TO HAVE FUN & WIN AT THE SAME TIME *Bill Talbert*	3.00

WILSHIRE PET LIBRARY

___ DOG TRAINING MADE EASY & FUN *John W. Kellogg*	5.00
___ HOW TO BRING UP YOUR PET DOG *Kurt Unkelbach*	2.00
___ HOW TO RAISE & TRAIN YOUR PUPPY *Jeff Griffen*	5.00

The books listed above can be obtained from your book dealer or directly from Melvin Powers. When ordering, please remit $2.00 postage for the first book and $1.00 for each additional book.

Melvin Powers
12015 Sherman Road, No. Hollywood, California 91605

HOW TO GET RICH IN MAIL ORDER
by Melvin Powers

1. How to Develop Your Mail Order Expertise 2. How to Find a Unique Product or Servic to Sell 3. How to Make Money with Classified Ads 4. How to Make Money with Display Ac 5. The Unlimited Potential for Making Money with Direct Mail 6. How to Copycat Successfn Mail Order Operations 7. How I Created A Best Seller Using the Copycat Technique 8. Ho to Start and Run a Profitable Mail Order, Special Interest Book or Record Business 9. I Enjc Selling Books by Mail – Some of My Successful and Not-So-Successful Ads and Direct Ma Circulars 10. Five of My Most Successful Direct Mail Pieces That Sold and Are Still Sellin Millions of Dollars Worth of Books 11. Melvin Powers' Mail Order Success Strategy – Follo It and You'll Become a Millionaire 12. How to Sell Your Products to Mail Order Companie Retail Outlets, Jobbers, and Fund Raisers for Maximum Distribution and Profits 13. How t Get Free Display Ads and Publicity That Can Put You on the Road to Riches 14. How to Mak Your Advertising Copy Sizzle to Make You Wealthy 15. Questions and Answers to Help Yo Get Started Making Money in Your Own Mail Order Business 16. A Personal Word fro Melvin Powers 17. How to Get Started Making Money in Mail Order. 18. Selling Produc on Television - An Exciting Challenge   8½"x11" — 352 Pages...$20.0

HOW TO SELF-PUBLISH YOUR BOOK AND HAVE THE FUN AND EXCITEMENT OF BEING A BEST-SELLING AUTHOR
by Melvin Powers

An expert's step-by-step guide to successfully marketing your book   240 Pages...$20.0

A NEW GUIDE TO RATIONAL LIVING
by Albert Ellis, Ph.D. & Robert A. Harper, Ph.D.

1. How Far Can You Go With Self-Analysis? 2. You Feel the Way You Think 3. Feeling Well t Thinking Straight 4. How You Create Your Feelings 5. Thinking Yourself Out of Emotion. Disturbances 6. Recognizing and Attacking Neurotic Behavior 7. Overcoming the Influence of the Past 8. Does Reason Always Prove Reasonable? 9. Refusing to Feel Desperatel Unhappy 10. Tackling Dire Needs for Approval 11. Eradicating Dire Fears of Failu 12. How to Stop Blaming and Start Living 13. How to Feel Undepressed though Frustrate 14. Controlling Your Own Destiny 15. Conquering Anxiety   256 Pages...$7.0

PSYCHO-CYBERNETICS
A New Technique for Using Your Subconscious Power
by Maxwell Maltz, M.D., F.I.C.S.

1. The Self Image: Your Key to a Better Life 2. Discovering the Success Mechanism Withi You 3. Imagination–The First Key to Your Success Mechanism 4. Dehypnotize Yourse from False Beliefs 5. How to Utilize the Power of Rational Thinking 6. Relax and Let Yo Success Mechanism Work for You 7. You Can Acquire the Habit of Happiness 8. Ingredien of the Success-Type Personality and How to Acquire Them 9. The Failure Mechanism: Ho to Make It Work For You Instead of Against You 10. How to Remove Emotional Scars, How to Give Yourself an Emotional Face Lift 11. How to Unlock Your Real Personalit 12. Do-It-Yourself Tranquilizers   288 Pages...$7.0

A PRACTICAL GUIDE TO SELF-HYPNOSIS
by Melvin Powers

1. What You Should Know About Self-Hypnosis 2. What About the Dangers of Hypnosi 3. Is Hypnosis the Answer? 4. How Does Self-Hypnosis Work? 5. How to Arouse Yourse from the Self-Hypnotic State 6. How to Attain Self-Hypnosis 7. Deepening the Self-Hypnot State 8. What You Should Know About Becoming an Excellent Subject 9. Techniques f Reaching the Somnambulistic State 10. A New Approach to Self-Hypnosis When All El Fails 11. Psychological Aids and Their Function 12. The Nature of Hypnosis 13. Practic Applications of Self-Hypnosis   128 Pages...$5.0

The books listed above can be obtained from your book dealer or directly from Melvin Power When ordering, please remit $2.00 postage for the first book and $1.00 for each additional boo

Melvin Powers
12015 Sherman Road, No. Hollywood, California 91605

WILSHIRE HORSE LOVERS' LIBRARY

___ AMATEUR HORSE BREEDER A. C. Leighton Hardman	5.00
___ AMERICAN QUARTER HORSE IN PICTURES Margaret Cabel Self	5.00
___ APPALOOSA HORSE Donna & Bill Richardson	7.00
___ ARABIAN HORSE Reginald S. Summerhays	5.00
___ ART OF WESTERN RIDING Suzanne Norton Jones	7.00
___ BASIC DRESSAGE Jean Froissard	5.00
___ BEGINNER'S GUIDE TO HORSEBACK RIDING Sheila Wall	5.00
___ BEHAVIOR PROBLEMS IN HORSES—HOW TO CURE THEM Susan McBane	12.00
___ BITS—THEIR HISTORY, USE AND MISUSE Louis Taylor	7.00
___ BREAKING & TRAINING THE DRIVING HORSE Doris Ganton	10.00
___ BREAKING YOUR HORSE'S BAD HABITS W. Dayton Sumner	10.00
___ COMPLETE TRAINING OF HORSE AND RIDER Colonel Alois Podhajsky	10.00
___ DISORDERS OF THE HORSE & WHAT TO DO ABOUT THEM E. Hanauer	5.00
___ DOG TRAINING MADE EASY & FUN John W. Kellogg	5.00
___ DRESSAGE—A STUDY OF THE FINER POINTS IN RIDING Henry Wynmalen	7.00
___ DRIVE ON Doris Ganton	7.00
___ DRIVING HORSES Sallie Walrond	5.00
___ EQUITATION Jean Froissard	7.00
___ FIRST AID FOR HORSES Dr. Charles H. Denning, Jr.	5.00
___ FUN ON HORSEBACK Margaret Cabell Self	4.00
___ HORSE DISEASES—CAUSES, SYMPTOMS & TREATMENT Dr. H. G. Belschner	7.00
___ HORSE OWNER'S CONCISE GUIDE Elsie V. Hanauer	5.00
___ HORSE SELECTION & CARE FOR BEGINNERS George H. Conn	10.00
___ HORSEBACK RIDING FOR BEGINNERS Louis Taylor	7.00
___ HORSEBACK RIDING MADE EASY & FUN Sue Henderson Coen	7.00
___ HORSES—THEIR SELECTION, CARE & HANDLING Margaret Cabell Self	5.00
___ HUNTER IN PICTURES Margaret Cabell Self	2.00
___ ILLUSTRATED BOOK OF THE HORSE S. Sidney (8½" x 11")	10.00
___ ILLUSTRATED HORSE TRAINING Captain M. H. Hayes	7.00
___ ILLUSTRATED HORSEBACK RIDING FOR BEGINNERS Jeanne Mellin	5.00
___ KNOW ALL ABOUT HORSES Harry Disston	5.00
___ LAME HORSE—CAUSES, SYMPTOMS & TREATMENT Dr. James R. Rooney	7.00
___ LAW & YOUR HORSE Edward H. Greene	7.00
___ POLICE HORSES Judith Campbell	2.00
___ PRACTICAL GUIDE TO HORSESHOEING	5.00
___ PRACTICAL HORSE PSYCHOLOGY Moyra Williams	7.00
___ PROBLEM HORSES—GUIDE FOR CURING SERIOUS BEHAVIOR HABITS Summerhays	5.00
___ REINSMAN OF THE WEST—BRIDLES & BITS Ed Connell	7.00
___ RIDE WESTERN Louis Taylor	7.00
___ SCHOOLING YOUR YOUNG HORSE George Wheatley	5.00
___ STABLE MANAGEMENT FOR THE OWNER-GROOM George Wheatley	7.00
___ STALLION MANAGEMENT—A GUIDE FOR STUD OWNERS A. C. Hardman	5.00
___ TEACHING YOUR HORSE TO JUMP W. J. Froud	5.00
___ YOU AND YOUR PONY Pepper Mainwaring Healey (8½" x 11")	6.00
___ YOUR PONY BOOK Hermann Wiederhold	2.00

The books listed above can be obtained from your book dealer or directly from Melvin Powers. When ordering, please remit $2.00 postage for the first book and $1.00 for each additional book.

Melvin Powers
12015 Sherman Road, No. Hollywood, California 91605

Notes

Notes

Notes